Praise for
There's No Place Like Working From Home

"As someone who has worked from a home office for over 30 years, I promise that you will increase your productivity, profit, and peace if you implement the advice that Elaine Quinn offers in *There's No Place Like Working From Home!*"

Barbara Hemphill
Author, *Taming the Paper Tiger*
ThePaperTiger.com

"I have worked from home for a number of years and was delighted to read Elaine Quinn's *There's No Place Like Working From Home*. I found her book to be clear, concise and practical, from the location and configuration of the office environment to loneliness, from paper filing to computer organization. She addresses all aspects of working from home. Her straightforward approach simplifies this type of business. The book is loaded with common sense directions to keep you from feeling overwhelmed and to help you develop a rhythm for working effectively and loving what you do. Great book!"

Mary Jo Cappitelli
Paralegal/Independent Contractor

"Whether you've been working from home for a while and struggling with organization and time management, or just starting out, get a copy of Elaine Quinn's book *There's No Place Like Working From Home*. Lots of good ideas, and it's an easy read, written in an engaging conversational style with humor and understanding."

Susan Kousek
Certified Professional Organizer® & Owner of Balanced Spaces®, LLC
BalancedSpaces.com

"The suggestions and tips offered in *There's No Place Like Working From Home* are insightful and easy to implement. I feel so much more productive and happier in my home office after following the advice in the book. Anyone who works from home...or is thinking about working from home...needs this book!"

Kathy Werhan
Author, Coach, and Speaker
KathyWerhan.com

"You're racking up billable hours while waiting for the cable guy in your sweats. Does it get any better? Actually, it could. Working from home does have some pitfalls and Quinn deftly identifies and addresses them in this quick and helpful read. Sharing not only common sense time-saving tips and basic IT techniques, but also dealing with less obvious issues such as motivation, isolation and maintaining that competitive edge when there's no one around to measure your performance, *"There's No Place Like Working From Home"* is a great reference for former corporate types who no longer have accustomed resources and personnel at their disposal."

Caryn Green
Digital Media Consultant

"There's No Place Like Working from Home is a must-have for anyone who has a home-based business. Elaine Quinn identifies common traps and challenges that plague work-from-home business owners and presents simple, easy-to-use solutions, many of which can be implemented immediately at no cost. Quinn clearly gets that when you're organized, it's easier to stay motivated and be productive!"

Lynne R. Sherman, Ph.D.
CEO, People Centered Solutions
DrLynneSherman.com

"I appreciate Elaine Quinn's "holistic" approach in *There's No Place Like Working from Home*. She addresses the unique organizational and logistical challenges of being effective and motivated in a home office environment. And she also gets to the hidden issues at the heart of the matter—the relationship between environment and motivation! Elaine understands that your space affects how you feel; and that's a critical "aha" for all who are seeking a healthy balance between work and life."

Anita Birsa
Design Solutions Interior Decor & Organization

"There's No Place Like Working from Home makes molehills out of mountains. Mountains of paper, mountains of email, mountains of 'to do' items—no problem! Everything has its place and time. This book shows you how to organize your time and space so tasks get done on schedule and done right, but in their proper order. This book puts *you* in the driver's seat."

Denise C. Thompson
Lector Training & Development
GreatLectors.com

There's No Place Like
Working From **Home**

There's No Place Working From Like Home

Get Organized
Stay Motivated
Get Things Done!

Elaine Quinn

CALLORAN

Chicago, IL

Published by Calloran Publishing
Chicago, IL

Copyright © 2011 Elaine Quinn

Cover Design © 2011 Imagine! Studios™
www.artsimagine.com

Cartoons © Randy Glasbergen. Reprinted with Permission.
www.glasbergen.com

First Calloran Publishing printing, July 2011

ISBN: 978-0-9833235-3-2
Library of Congress Control Number: 2011911622

Table of Contents

Acknowledgments

I would like to give special thanks to the people who helped me get this book out of my heart and into the real world.

> To my husband and best friend, Bob Andresen, whose love, patience, writing skills, and creativity accompanied me throughout the entire project.

> To my friends Sandra Younger, Kathy Werhan, Lynne Sherman, Marlene Tilsner, and Elaine Kokai for their encouragement, confidence, and editorial recommendations.

> To Kristen Eckstein, who guided me and managed the editorial, design, and production phases of bringing the book to life.

> To the many, many clients I've worked with over the years, for helping me to understand and appreciate the unique needs of the work-from-home professional, and to discover and implement practical ways to address them.

> To my mother, whose love and support made all things possible.

Introduction
The Work-From-Home Revolution

"For those of you headed to the office, today's forecast calls for scattered frustration, followed by a brief storm of criticism and a flurry of random distractions."

Remind me again, why is it I keep going there?

There's a revolution under way in today's workplace. Yesterday's rigid nine-to-five office routine is losing ground to the enticing option of working from home. About forty-two million people—roughly one-third of the U.S. workforce—now work from home at least one or two days a week. And no wonder. Working from home saves time and money, reduces commuting, eases childcare challenges, and offers tremendous flexibility and freedom. Of course, it also comes with challenges. Success depends on knowing the landscape and overcoming the obstacles.

If you're part of the work-from-home trend, this book is for you. It's designed to be especially helpful for:

> Solopreneurs—consultants, writers, artists, designers, and other solo professionals

> People who want to work more productively while maintaining a healthful life balance, allowing plenty of time for family and outside interests

> People looking for help in meeting the challenges of working from home

As you read, you'll learn how the workplace has evolved to support the work-from-home revolution. You'll be reminded of the many reasons to love working from home, along with ways to recognize and overcome the common challenges faced by work-from-home professionals. Plus, you'll find loads of tips, tricks, and bright ideas to help you avoid the primary pitfalls that cause so many new businesses to fail: lack of organizational skills, procrastination and poor time management, dwindling motivation, and lack of work/life balance.

Who's working from home and why?

Today's growing numbers of work-from-home professionals came to the decision to leave a traditional workplace for different reasons—some by choice, others by chance after losing a regular job because of lay-offs, restructuring, or outsourcing. Overall, they fall into three categories:

1. **The self-employed, those working by themselves, for themselves.** As more and more companies have downsized or even capsized, many employees inclined to strike out on their own have decided now is a good time to do it. The increasing feasibility and appeal of owning a business have also contributed to the recent explosion of entrepreneurship. Almost seven million people—more than 5 percent of the U.S. working population—own a home-based business. Many are former corporate workers who grew tired of corporate pressures and politics. Others are second-career retirees who now consult based on their former work experience or have turned a personal interest into a business. Most are service-oriented professionals.

2. **Employees for companies located elsewhere.** Technology and cultural acceptance have also made it possible for company workers to work from home. About a third of employees at private, for-profit companies now work from home one or more days a week. They may be outside sales representatives or service personnel responsible for a specific product line or geographic region. Or they may be telecommuters who have negotiated a part-time or full-time arrangement with their employers.

3. **Employees whose work overflows from their day jobs.** Many employees find their workdays consistently overflow into what used to be "personal" time. For many, corporate downsizing has resulted in heavier workloads, to the point that they can no longer get everything done during a normal workday. Working from home has become a regular part of their evenings and/or weekends.

How did working from home become so prevalent?

Today's workplace revolution is definitely a product of our times. At least seven twenty-first-century trends and conditions have converged to make it possible.

1. **The nature of business has changed.** Traditional office procedures were created at a time when few people owned their own businesses or worked from home. Virtually all companies employed secretaries who handled office administration—taking phone calls and messages, keeping appointment calendars, and following up on work in progress. Secretaries created documents, then designed and managed the filing systems that housed them. With the introduction of personal computers, it became easier to create our own documents, manage our own files and calendars, and handle our own recordkeeping than to explain to a secretary what we needed. Pretty soon, it was *expected* that we would do these things ourselves. Next, secretaries disappeared altogether. Now that a battered economy has forced people to re-think their work situations, many have thought, "I've been doing all my own work anyway; why don't I take what I've learned on my job and start my own business."

2. **Technology allows it.** Thanks to modern technology and the Internet, the barriers to self-employment and small business ownership have all but disappeared. Better, smaller, faster, less expensive office equipment suitable for home offices is readily available. Cell phones allow us to conduct phone calls, receive e-mail and stay in touch anywhere. Powerful laptop computers make practically the entire office portable. A huge selection of business software brings every conceivable business function to our fingertips. And the Internet allows business to be conducted without regard to geography.

3. **Corporate jobs are no longer secure.** The likelihood of spending an entire career with one company has dwindled. Many professionals today have lost jobs to downsizing, mergers, or business failures. Others have seen their jobs disappear because of outsourcing, technological changes, productivity improvements, and flattened corporate organization charts. Many have been unable to find new jobs with equivalent pay or status. These shaky corporate prospects make starting a home-based business seem more reasonable than ever before.

4. **Self-employed independent contractors are picking up the slack.** Although corporate cost cutting has eliminated many employees, it's increased opportunities for freelancers. Businesses can procure high-quality work from independent contractors without the long-term commitments employees require. Also, as more people start their own businesses, they're reaching out to one another for help with tasks they're not good at, don't enjoy, or simply don't have time to do.

5. **The "services" segment of the economy remains robust.** Despite the recent economic downturn, there's great and growing demand for both business and personal services to meet the needs of busy people with complicated lives. Consumers who have less and less time are willing to pay for expertise and quality help. Service jobs can often be operated from home, keeping start-up costs and ongoing overhead low. They generally don't require product inventory, removing another cost barrier. Even services that do involve products often have them drop shipped directly from the manufacturer to the customer. There's no longer a need to personally warehouse and ship products.

6. **Family lifestyles have changed.** People today are less willing than before to sacrifice time with their families. They're tired of the cost, time-sink, and frustration of commuting. Two incomes have become necessary to support most Americans' lifestyle expectations. Yet, the net gain from that second income is severely reduced by the costs of working outside the home. At the same time, the typical American home has increased in size over the past few decades. Today's larger homes often include space that can be converted into an office. Thanks to the Internet and today's advanced technology, most work-from-home professionals can conduct business anywhere. So if the family decides to relocate, the home business can go right along.

7. **Our culture has changed.** Owning your own business has acquired a certain "cool" image. People are less dependent than in years past on the prestige of working for a "brand-name" company. Few young people expect or want to spend their entire working lives within one company, or even within one industry. Young people are marrying later, giving them more time to pursue their entrepreneurial dreams without the pressure of having to support a family. Among dual-income couples, one partner may be able to pursue an entrepreneurial interest, while the other provides a steady income with benefits. Responding to these changes, many colleges and universities now offer programs or degrees in entrepreneurism. These trends are continuing to pick up momentum; the more small business ownership success is publicized, the more people are encouraged to try it.

What's so great about working from home?

The appeal of working from home is undeniable, especially if you're in business for yourself. Consider these advantages:

1. **Work at what you love.** When you have your own business, you choose your line of work and which aspects of it you want to concentrate on. You pick your business model, create your goals, and decide on priorities. You select which projects you work on and which people you work with. If a business relationship doesn't work out, you can decide to end it. And all your hard work goes into something that you actually own.

2. **Be your "true" self.** Working for yourself means you can be yourself, without the limitation of having to fit into a specific corporate culture. You can free your personality, individuality, and creativity and find clients who value those qualities.

3. **Work on your own terms.** Your career is no longer dependent on corporate rules or politics. You set your own rules. Make your own decisions. Decide your own work schedule. Develop your own processes and results. Create your own working environment. Dress as you please. Listen to your favorite music. Bring your pets to work with you.

4. **Develop a broad range of business skills, if you wish.** As an entrepreneur your work is varied since you do everything yourself. You manage all the resources, vendors, clients, and so on. You can do something different every day if that brings you greater job satisfaction.

5. **Avoid certain tasks, if you wish.** Do the things you like to do and are good at, and outsource the rest to others who do it better.

6. **Determine your own income.** As an entrepreneur, you can determine if and how much you want to grow your business. Business growth depends on the value you provide to your clients. If you want to make more money, acquire more clients and/or provide more value to them. As a business owner, you'll be compensated based on your own talents, skills, and efforts, rather than on political maneuvering. You won't have to worry about being laid off if business is down, or being fired by a bad boss. And if you hit a home run, you'll collect all the profits.

7. **Enjoy a flexible schedule and work location.** Few work-at-home professionals keep traditional business hours. Your time may be dictated to some degree by your customers' schedules, but other than that you control when and where you work. You can schedule around your priorities—community, family, school, professional or personal development. You can work from home, from a local coffee shop, from your car, or from your hotel when you travel. It doesn't matter as long as you have a cell phone, laptop and Internet access.

8. **Spend more time with your family.** Be more involved in their lives. Being there when your children come home from school makes it easier to get to know their friends, too, since they can invite them over.

9. **Eliminate commuting.** Though you may travel to clients' locations, you don't have to spend time every day commuting, dealing with traffic congestion, stress, and frustration. By eliminating a thirty-minute commute to and from your workplace each day, you could

save the equivalent of five and a half weeks over the course of a year! You can get more work done in the time you would have spent commuting, or use that time for other pursuits. Save money, too, on gas, car repairs, insurance, parking, or public transportation.

10. **Be more productive**. Studies show that employees working from home actually increase productivity compared with those working in traditional workplaces. Estimates are that in most businesses 25 percent to 30 percent of employee time is wasted chatting with coworkers, taking breaks, and doing nonessential activities.

11. **Save money**. Working from home significantly reduces expenses. You don't have to pay for office space. If you've used a housecleaning or a lawn care service in the past, you can do that work yourself using the time you saved by *not* commuting. Most of the time you can wear casual clothing rather than a fancy wardrobe that requires dry-cleaning. Instead of expensive restaurant lunches, you can eat at home. You're also less likely to rely on pre-packaged meals or fast food at dinnertime. Further, with a room in your home dedicated exclusively to business, you can claim a proportion of rent/mortgage and utilities on your tax return.

12. **Define work/life satisfaction on your own terms**. Decide when and how much time you'll devote to the various aspects of your life. You choose when you need to work and when your family comes first.

What adjustments can work-from-home professionals expect?

Work-from-home professionals generally agree that the advantages far outweigh the challenges, but those who succeed, especially those who choose to work for themselves, must make adjustments to accommodate their new working style. Despite all its benefits, working from home is still a real job and it's still real work.

It's a very different reality from a traditional work environment with its bosses, coworkers, and routines. When you work from home, there's no one on site to help shoulder the workload, to turn to when you have a question, or call on when your computer crashes.

Many people discover that their new unstructured workday makes it difficult to get things done and hard to stay on top of the tasks and information they need to manage. It's easy to feel stressed, isolated, burned out, conflicted about family vs. work issues, and have difficulty staying motivated.

I'm not trying to discourage you in any way; I just want you know in advance what to expect and how to adjust your expectations and attitudes.

What do people miss most when they begin working from home?

> **The sense of identity that comes with holding a title and role in an organization.** When you work for yourself, there's no "borrowed" prestige from your employer's reputation, no structured hierarchy to give weight to your job title, no management recognition, achievement awards or promotions, no support departments or mentoring relationships.

> **Accountability.** No one prompts you to get going in the morning. No one knows if you're accomplishing your goals or not. There's no good-natured competitive pressure from your peers spurring you to perform at your peak and no performance reviews or candid evaluations of your work or progress. You may miss

this type of self-affirming or self-improvement feedback.

> **The social network**. Many work-from-home professionals miss long-term, collaborative social relationships and camaraderie with colleagues. Even if you remain friends with former coworkers, you lose touch because you're no longer included in their everyday talk about what's going on. There's no natural mental and social break as you meet others for coffee or lunch and no built-in support network to share your frustrations and encourage you through difficulties.

> **Idea input from others**. When you work on your own, there's no access to more experienced coworkers, no new ideas coming from what others are doing, no comfortable peer group to bounce around ideas or exchange advice with, no collaborative energy. Your knowledge and skills can become outdated.

What's new and different about working from home?

> **Learning to run a business.** Small business owners are usually experts in their field but inexperienced in planning, launching, and managing a profitable business. Many lack the knowledge and research time required to make decisions about non-core issues. Some may not even realize there are skills they lack. Plus, the time and cost for additional training must come out of their own limited resources.

> **Bearing complete financial responsibility.** When you run your own business, finding a steady stream of clients to create income is up to you. And of course all the expenses are yours, too. The cost of outfitting

a home office can be considerable. Every decision requires a cost/benefit analysis; a trade-off between time and money. You may be tempted to get by with inadequate equipment or processes that actually reduce effectiveness and efficiency. You may also have to do without the latest whiz-bang technology that would normally be provided to you by an employer.

> **Having to do everything yourself.** Solopreneurs quickly learn that if you don't do it, it doesn't get done. If you don't know how to do something, you either have to learn how or find someone who already knows. When you do outsource, finding reliable support for marketing, IT, PR, etc., is time consuming and mostly by trial and error. All the decisions are yours; you have to research everything yourself. It can seem there are not enough hours in the day.

> **Establishing a suitable home office.** Since a home office is often an afterthought it may be necessary to upgrade wiring, electrical outlets, lighting, etc., to create a workspace where you can be productive. If at all possible, you need a separate room located away from family traffic patterns, a place quiet enough to concentrate and hold private telephone conversations. You also need to equip your office with appropriate furnishings, adequate equipment, and sufficient supplies. And of course all these costs come out of your own pocket.

> **Staying organized.** If you don't possess or develop strong organizing skills, sooner or later you'll have big problems. If you don't create procedures for dealing with incoming information, you'll drown. A cluttered work space and disorganized files will cost you valuable time and energy (and your professional image) as you search for lost documents. Poor time-man-

agement skills will frustrate you and keep you from accomplishing your goals. Missed deadlines, forgotten commitments and the like will anger clients and doom your business.

> **Feeling socially isolated.** Once a work-from-home business is up and running, most solo professionals find their world filled with customers, suppliers, and business associates. But if you're accustomed to being with others all day, it can be very lonely when you first start to work alone. Again, many solopreneurs miss the professional and personal camaraderie of the workplace.

> **Difficulty staying on task.** People who work from home often report that self-discipline becomes a major issue because of distractions, interruptions, and temptations. You may be tempted to join in family activities when you should be working. Children may need attention. Friends and neighbors will call, make requests, or send invitations your way since you're at home "anyway." It's surprisingly hard for them to understand that you're at home *working*. And it's hard to avoid being distracted by household chores when they're right in front of you. The laundry, the vacuuming, the yard, the errands—there's always something available to keep you from working! At home, background noise may keep you from concentrating fully. Then there's the constant temptation of the Internet. A quick peek at the news can turn into an hour of browsing. Finally, there's always a kitchen just down the hall. Those who snack too frequently can easily lose time *and* gain weight!

> **Maintaining a professional image.** Not long ago, the statement "I work from home" raised eyebrows. People assumed you didn't have a job and had taken

to calling yourself a "consultant" because you were embarrassed to tell the truth and say you were unemployed. Today, so many people work from home that few people give it a second thought. Still, it's smart to be aware of issues that could detract from the professional image you want to convey. You'll need to establish a website, have business cards printed, and eliminate family noise in the background when you're on a business call. And you'll want to look presentable whenever you leave the house, because it's on those days when you look your worst that you're most likely to run into clients or potential clients.

> **Defining work/life boundaries.** When home is where the office is, it's hard to separate the two. Besides, when you love your work, you may be happy to work until all hours of the night. On the other hand, you want and need to be considerate of the other people in your life. It's a dilemma for which there's no pat answer. Solo professionals need to work out arrangements they and their family are comfortable with.

> **Staying motivated.** Once the glow of a new business has worn off and the realities of everyday hard work set in, some people lose enthusiasm. Initial expectations of the entrepreneur lifestyle can be unrealistic, especially for those without significant business experience. Being suddenly on your own to handle all aspects of a business can be overwhelming when times get tough. Customers care only about results; few know or appreciate the hard work required to achieve them.

These issues are so common that by mentioning some of them here, I want to reassure you that you are not alone. In this book, we'll discuss solutions for all of these challenges.

Working from home is not for everyone. It's still a real job, and you still have to work! But if you're committed, disciplined, and self-motivated, you can't beat the advantages. Millions of people have learned to successfully work from home—and so can you!

Part I
GET ORGANIZED

**Set up a workspace
that's efficient, effective,
and convenient**

What's Getting Organized All About?

"Organized people are just people who are too lazy to look for things!"

It seems lost items are always found in the last place we look for them. Why don't we save time and just look for them in the **last** *place in the* **first** *place?*

Why is it so hard to keep your office organized?

I f you have trouble getting organized, you're not alone. In every annual poll about New Year's resolutions, people admit that next to losing weight, getting organized is their highest priority. They're especially concerned about their offices!

People often ask me "Why can't I seem to keep my office organized?"

The answer may be that they don't have the time. Or the interest. Or the skills. Some people put "getting organized" at the bottom of their priority list until their clutter is out of control. Then they get overwhelmed. Instead of focusing on one small area at a time, they look at the entire room and see such a mess they don't know where to start. So they don't start at all.

But behind these reasons, there's something else. Something you may not have thought much about.

Times Have Changed

Now, even in corporate offices, there's no longer a person whose sole purpose is to organize and manage the office and the work of its inhabitants. Everyone but the top tier of executives is expected to be self-sufficient. Even though we've never been taught the skills, we expect ourselves to tend to our core business *and* manage administrative and organizing tasks as well. No wonder we can't keep up!

Habits Haven't Changed

Inertia is a powerful force and habits are hard to break. Despite the fact that we now use computers to create almost all business communication, we're still in the habit of wanting to see things *on paper*. People print out e-mails and other documents, creating unnecessary paper that clogs filing systems. Even after a project is completed, inactive files remain in drawers where they take up space and make it difficult to find the *active* files we're looking for.

Now, in addition to paper, workers accumulate computer clutter! Hundreds of e-mails and other documents tend to remain in the system though they're no longer needed. As with paper, searching through hundreds of outdated computer files to find the one you want is frustrating, inefficient, and a huge time-waster.

Unfortunately, it's easier to keep doing the same old thing than it is to change, even when you *want* to change. But as American self-help author and success coach Tony Robbins, says, "If you do what you've always done, you'll get what you've always gotten." And if what you've always had is a *messy* office, it requires learning new habits in order to have an *organized* one.

What could being disorganized cost you?

I'm sure you've heard it said many times, "People do business with those they know, like, and trust." **Ob**taining clients may be largely a matter of personality, but to **re**tain them they have to trust that you'll deliver what you say you will. In today's economy, you can't afford to be disorganized. If you miss deadlines, run projects over budget, and behave in an inconsiderate manner you won't get repeat business.

Take a look at this list of questions. If you answer "yes" to any one of them, you're in danger of being disorganized, and that could be costing you a lot more than you might think.

Money Down the Drain?

> Have you had to pay a penalty because you overlooked a bill that was due?

> Have you missed out on a product rebate because you lost the receipt?

> Have you had gift cards or store credits expire because you forgot about them?

> Have you bought a duplicate of something you already had but couldn't find?

Professional Embarrassment?

> Have you failed to deliver exactly what was asked for because you overlooked an important piece of information?

> Are you reluctant to invite someone to your office because it's a mess?

> Have you lost credibility with a client due to a missed deadline?

> Do your workdays seem to disappear before you've gotten much accomplished?

> Are your business goals and priorities a little unclear?

Substandard Performance?

> Does your disorganized office suggest sloppy work standards?

> Would *you* feel confident in doing business with someone whose office looked like yours?

Missed Opportunities?

> Have you failed to follow up on promising business leads?

> Are you without a system for managing the contact information of people you meet at networking events?

> Have you ever declined a business meeting because you didn't feel prepared?

Wasted Time?

> Do you frequently have to search for something you know you have but can't find?

> Do you often have to backtrack because you forgot something?

> Have you allowed yourself to be distracted by items on your desk when you had something important to do?

Damaged Relationships?

> Have you been late to an important meeting because you couldn't find your keys or misplaced the directions?

> Have you appeared inconsiderate by forgetting an important event?

> Have you upset a colleague because you borrowed something and couldn't find it to return it?

> Are the long hours you're working keeping you from your friends and family?

Emotional Stress?

> When you're facing a deadline do you wait until the last minute, and then panic because you can't find something you need?

> Do you sometimes feel you've forgotten something important but can't remember what it is?

> Have you ever agreed to take on a project you really didn't have time for?

> Does your being disorganized annoy and irritate others?

When colleagues work together on a project, if one disorganized person misses a deadline it jeopardizes the reputation of everyone involved. And with independent small business owners usually there's no warning, unlike in a large business office where you can monitor progress. Don't let that disorganized person be *you*, and be wary of others whose disorganized habits could end up costing you business!

How could being better organized help you?

Since people do business with those they know, like, and trust, wouldn't you like to be that kind of person? Being known and liked are largely a matter of getting out there and getting along with those you meet. That's why networking groups are so popular and effective. It's an easy way for clients to connect with you and give your business a try. But being *trusted*—that's something else.

To get repeat business you have to do what you say you'll do. You have to pay attention to the little things that make a difference, and getting better organized will help with that. Being better organized will not only help you gain the trust of potential repeat customers, it will also improve everything about the way you manage your business. Being better organized is definitely a habit worth acquiring!

Let's flip the previous list of questions around and see how you would answer this version.

Spend Money Wisely

> Would you like to have a reminder system you could trust so you're never late paying bills?

> How much money could you save if you could always find receipts needed for rebates or returns?

> How much could you save if you were reminded of your gift cards and store credits at the moment you were about to buy something?

Present a Professional Image

> Wouldn't you like to feel confident you'll finish a project on time because you worked out in advance how much time each step would take?

> How great would it be to know you can invite a client to your office any time because it's always presentable?

> How much business do you think you would get if you had the reputation of always being "on time and on budget?"

> What if you made conscious decisions about priorities so you could get the most important tasks completed each day?

Capitalize On Opportunities

> How much more money could you make if you had a reliable follow-up system to keep in touch with clients and potential business partners?

> Wouldn't you like to have time to prepare adequately for important meetings?

Save Time

> How about having your files and office paperwork in order and so you could quickly find what you're looking for?

> What if you had a way to remind yourself of tasks you needed to take care of?

> How much time would you save if you could concentrate on the task at hand and just get it done?

Preserve Relationships

> How much more relaxed and effective would you be if you were always on time for meetings and didn't have to make excuses?

> Would you like a system that reminded you of important dates and events?

> Wouldn't you love colleagues to know without a doubt they could depend on you to follow through on commitments?

> What if you could get your work done and still have time for a personal life?

Reduce Stress

> What if your work were so organized that you met deadlines without a problem?

> Would you like to have checklists for important procedures so you never forget something important?

> Would you like to have a graceful way to decline projects you really don't have time for?

> How much would your confidence improve if you felt fully in charge of your workload?

There's a huge difference in the way you feel reading these two lists, right? Wouldn't you like to see yourself in the second list rather than the first? It's possible for anyone to become better organized. Some people hold misconceptions about organizing, though. Let me clear up some of those.

Common misconceptions about organizing

Being organized is a character trait that you either have or you don't.

It's not a moral failing if you're not organized! It's merely a skill you haven't acquired. While people vary in their natural tendencies, anyone can learn to be organized.

A hectic schedule, constant interruptions, and emergencies make it impossible to stay organized.

Some people believe that being disorganized is inevitable if they're busy. However, working environments, schedules, and habits can usually be modified to reduce interruptions and distractions. A few changes can enable you to focus and get the important things done.

Getting better organized requires too much time.

Some people think that being "organized" is too time consuming. But the truth is that once you're organized you'll actually save time because you'll be able to find things easily. You won't have to repeatedly "get organized;" you simply return items to their designated spaces.

Spend your time wisely. Like any investment, a small effort now will pay big dividends later. It is better to get *fewer* important things done than to get *many* unimportant things done.

Organizing is boring.

Many disorganized people are very bright, with lots of interests. Sometimes that's exactly *why* they're disorganized! They don't stay focused on any one thing long enough to get much accomplished. However, being organized can allow you to pursue interests in a way that's truly enriching and satisfying, instead of superficially flitting from one activity to another.

If an office is neat, it's organized.

Being organized isn't only about clutter control. All your papers can be neatly stacked, but if you can't quickly find what you're looking for, they're not organized. Being organized is about more than paper management, too. It includes space management, project management, time management, and self management.

Once my office is organized, it will stay that way.

Being organized isn't a single event; it's an ongoing process. *Getting* organized will probably require a concentrated chunk of time. *Staying* organized requires a moderate amount of effort as you begin to establish new habits. *Being* organized requires a decision to take the time at regular intervals to practice those habits. Once they're established, and you realize your work is easier and more convenient, you won't want to allow those old habits to creep back in.

Being organized is *not*:

> **Being efficient**

  While being organized may help you to be efficient, there's more to it than that. Being *efficient* means accomplishing tasks without wasted time or effort. Being organized means that you identify goals, determine what tasks to do, and when to do them.

> **Being rigid or regimented**

  To the contrary, you're completely free to be spontaneous. When you're organized, you're aware of the status of your tasks and priorities, and can rearrange them whenever you decide to.

> **Wasting time "planning" instead of "doing"**

  It take less time and effort to be organized than not. It's less stressful and chaotic to think about what you're going to do and why, than to constantly run into unexpected issues that keep you from accomplishing your goals.

〉 A one-time event

Inertia is a powerful force. If you've had trouble keeping your office organized, you'll need to develop some new habits. And like any habit, that will take time. You won't become a different person overnight. Experts say it takes most people twenty-one repetitions to establish a new habit so give yourself time to change.

The truth is that organizing is a skill like any other and it's an important skill for small business owners to learn. In fact, it turns out to be a vital skill. Lack of organizational skills, including time management, is one of the ten most common reasons small businesses fail.

Why do small businesses fail?

It's no secret that a large majority of small businesses fail in the first few years. What happens, and what can you do to help ensure your business is not among them?

It's important to understand the kinds of problems that commonly arise and be prepared to avoid them or deal with them. Following are ten of the most common reasons small businesses don't make it. In this book you'll find in-depth discussions of reasons one through four, along with dozens of ideas on how to work through them. To minimize the chance that your business will be sunk by reasons five through ten, find and invest in professional business, financial, and marketing advice.

1. **Lack of organizational skills:** Many small business owners are experts in their industry. However, once you get past the specific knowledge and skills required, running a business is largely a matter of being organized. You need to have an efficient work space,

explicit goals, and a rational method for achieving them. You need to keep accurate and easily accessible records. You need prioritized to-do lists and an organized structure to your day so that you get the important things done. You need to manage your time effectively.

2. **Procrastination and poor time management:** When you're the Chief Everything Officer, you can't afford to waste time on unimportant tasks while critical tasks pile up. Putting off tasks you don't enjoy will sink your business faster than anything else. Your time management skills need to be sharp and you should always be thinking, "Is this the most productive use of my time right now?"

3. **Dwindling motivation:** Entrepreneurs often get excited about new ideas, but lose enthusiasm once they discover running a business isn't easy. Keeping a business afloat requires a huge investment of time, money, energy, and emotion. What will keep you interested and enjoying the hard work you'll have to keep doing long after the novelty has worn off?

4. **Intrusion on personal life.** It's easy to underestimate the effect the commitment to your business will have on the rest of your life. If you can't find some way to balance your business and personal life, both will suffer.

Other reasons include:

5. **Lack of business experience:** Some first-time business owners have unrealistic expectations. They're swept away by an idea or hobby they love and don't consider what it will take to turn it into a profit-making business. They're often not prepared to face rou-

tine business problems like vendor management and customer service issues.

6. **Poor planning:** Some small business owners neglect the formality of writing a business plan. A business plan helps bring your vision and goals clearly into focus, and identifies what strategies and tactics you'll need to realize them. Sometimes small business owners have just one product, one service, or one major client, and they have no backup plan in case something changes.

7. **Insufficient capital:** Most businesses are very slow to get off the ground. You need enough cash on hand to survive for at least a couple of years before the business starts generating income.

8. **Poor financial controls:** An important part of running a business is keeping financial and business records. You have to review your revenue and expense report each month, and you have to submit tax returns and other business-related filings. If you don't know how to do these, or don't want to, get help from someone who does.

9. **Ineffective sales and marketing:** It's important to have good marketing and sales instincts, experience, or professional advice. If you don't attract the right customers, even the best products and services won't sell.

10. **Bad location:** If your business is dependent on foot traffic or customer convenience, make sure your location fits the bill. Being near your suppliers helps, too.

Make the decision right now that you'll master the skills necessary for good organization and time management and you'll have more time to concentrate on the other factors that will make your business successful!

Make Your Workspace Work for You

"The key to working at home is the one that locks the bathroom door. That's the only place I can work without distractions!"

Where's the best place for your home office? Come to think of it, the bathroom might be perfect. It offers a place to sit, a bathtub to hold your files, and a roll of paper for note taking— all within easy reach!

I f you're going to *work* at home, rather than just *be* at home, you need to create an environment that will allow you to operate in a business-like manner.

There is no one "correct" way to set up your workspace. An organized office doesn't have to mean a desk with nothing on it and all paperwork hidden away in drawers with alphabetized files. If you forget about things unless you *see* them this clearly would not work for you. Instead, you should have project folders in an organizer on top of your desk where you'll see them all the time.

However, there's plenty of advice available from people who have tried all different kinds of work-from-home arrangements. Here's what they have to say.

Select the right location

A home-based business usually starts small, so the space allotted to it is often an afterthought. But when your business starts to grow it becomes inconvenient to go to the other side of the room every time you need to file something. Before you know it you have stacks of clutter on the floor waiting to be filed the next time you get up from your desk. Next, you decide that going to the closet each time you need something is a waste of time, so supplies end up all over your desk on a permanent basis.

When these things happen, you need to reconsider your office arrangement. Just like a child who has outgrown his clothes, your business may have outgrown its initial location. Here are a few things to keep in mind.

Find a place of your own

If at all possible, find a separate room for working purposes only. It's a convenient way to isolate yourself from the rest of the house while you focus on your work. When clients call, they shouldn't be aware that you're operating a business out of your home. Be professional and eliminate family background noise.

It's important for *you*, too. You need a clear distinction between work and home. That way, when you're in your office, you're in the right state of mind. When your office is no different from where you live, it's impossible to get away from work. Virtually *every* single work-from-home professional says that unless you live alone, trying to work on the couch or in the family room is a recipe for inefficiency. You'll give your work half the attention and twice the time it deserves.

Along those lines, I would caution you that working from a dining room table or similar makeshift setup is likely to be ineffective and inconvenient in the long run. It will be difficult to accomplish anything meaningful in the midst of family activity. Besides, you don't want to continually be relocating your work at dinnertime or when guests come over.

Not only will it be difficult to keep your work in order, but you'll also lose time trying to recover your train of thought when you resume. Not to mention the risk of important details or deadlines getting lost in transit.

Hide in plain sight

If you just don't have the space for a dedicated office you can have a home office that can be concealed when it's not in use. A reach-in closet can be converted into a mini-office by placing a two-drawer file cabinet at each end and a long counter on top. You can make the office literally disappear just by closing the doors if the room is needed for overnight guests.

Shelves can be installed above to hold supplies, notebooks, and the like. If you're lucky and the closet has a light, add a light socket outlet adapter plug and an extension cord and you've got electricity for your computer, printer, chargers, etc. And if you need additional work surfaces or storage beyond the closet, you can buy functional and attractive furnishings specifically designed and scaled for a home office.

Another alternative is an office armoire, whose doors can be closed to conceal your workspace. In most cases, however, an armoire won't provide enough room for anything but the smallest of businesses. This arrangement should be considered only temporary, but if your space is extremely limited this may be your only choice. Separating such a workspace from the rest of the room by a screen, bookcase, filing cabinet, or other divider will help keep it private.

Don't get caught in traffic

It's usually a good idea to locate your office away from major traffic patterns in your home. Constant noise and household activity will not only distract you, but also will sound unprofessional over the telephone. An ideal location would be an unused room that's not on the main floor. That could be a spare bedroom, an alcove off a hallway, or even a basement. In fact, a finished basement could be an ideal solution if it has good lighting and comfortable working conditions.

Some work-from-home parents like to have the office located where they can easily keep an eye on their children, even including a television so that on days the children are home from school they can join them in the office.

The main thing is to choose a place you'll want to be. I've seen beautifully furnished offices going unused because they were *too* isolated, cold, or inconvenient, and the business owner ending up working somewhere else entirely.

Consider convenience

If your work involves heavy boxes, samples, supplies, or other items that you constantly have to transport to and from your office, think about whether an office that's up or down a flight of stairs will be practical. No matter how much you love the idea of working in that cute little loft up the circular staircase, after a few weeks you're likely to decide it's just too much trouble!

Protect personal privacy

If clients visit you in your office, you'll want to choose a location for your office that's near an entrance to maintain some degree of privacy and professionalism. There's no need for visitors to be evaluating your choice of décor as they wander through your home. If they're likely to stay for any length of time, think about having a powder room nearby that's been cleared of personal belongings.

Decrease distractions

Plan work that requires concentration for a time when there's less activity in the house.

Consider posting a "Do Not Disturb" sign during working hours to remind family members not to interrupt unless it's truly important.

Arrange for someone to watch little ones. If you try to work and attend to your children at the same time you won't do a good job at either.

While some people feel that background noise helps them concentrate, be wary of televisions or other distracting equipment in the office.

Make it inviting

Your office should be a pleasant and comfortable environment with adequate space, lighting, and ventilation. It should be a place that makes you feel inspired, efficient, and productive. Don't be tempted to furnish it with leftovers that aren't welcome in the rest of the house. They likely won't meet your needs, and you won't feel good about working in a poorly furnished space. Having a professional-quality workspace is important if you're going to enjoy your work and produce professional-quality results.

Don't skimp on space

Choose a space large enough to create separate areas for different work functions such as computer, telephone, and paperwork. You'll need room to keep all the supplies needed for each activity together and convenient. For example, keep a message log and pen near the phone, so you're not fumbling around when a call comes in. Keep a replacement printer cartridge and a ream of paper near the printer, not across the room in the supply closet.

If you have papers to sort or printed materials to assemble into folders, equip your office with a table where you can do this work. For extensive reading, add a comfortable chair and good lighting. Your desk should be primarily for active work; if you try to read there you're likely to find it uncomfortable.

Create a convenient office layout

Your productivity will immediately increase if you arrange your office to be convenient. Making your office convenient begins with making it functional. This calls for a bit of thought about how you work and what tools and supplies you use the most. The principles to keep in mind when you lay out your office are the same as for organizing in general:

1. **Put things where you use them.**

Each work activity should have its own designated work zone where you have the space and materials you need to conduct that activity. Decide the most logical place to conduct each type of work, gather all the materials and supplies you need for that work, and arrange them conveniently in that zone.

> Place the phone where you can pick it up with your non-dominant hand. That way your dominant hand will be free to take notes. Even better, keep a wireless headset or earpiece handy and you'll be free to take notes, find files, or walk around.

> Put a pen and note pad near the phone so you can easily write things down.

> Store extra paper and printer cartridges near the printer.

> Keep instruction manuals next to the related piece of office equipment.

2. Put things you use most frequently closest to you.

> **On or in your desk:** telephone and contact list; "action" items like your to-do list and planner/calendar; current project files, tickler file, and everyday office supplies and accessories

> **Nearby:** computer, printer, and their supplies; checklists you use regularly; active files; frequently consulted references; recently completed projects

> **Somewhere in the office:** less frequently used equipment and supplies (cabinet or closet), software CDs and manuals (case or binder), books (shelf or bookcase), archived files (file drawers or CD cases)

3. Put things where you'll think to look for them.

> Place things where your instinct tells you to. If your first thought it to put everyday office supplies in the center drawer of your desk, put them there.

> Keep your tickler file in the drawer that seems most logical and convenient.

> Group similar products together—computer supplies together, paper goods together.

4. Put things where they'll work.

> Position your computer so that the screen doesn't reflect glare.

> Consider the location of cable and electrical outlets when placing your desk and equipment. If they don't match, have an electrician add what's needed.

Equip your office efficiently

An office that works efficiently is an office that's *functional*. As a bonus, you'll find that when it's *functional* it's also *organized*! Make sure the equipment in your office does what you need it to and you'll automatically be better organized. Think about the following points when you're outfitting your office.

Desk

Your desk will undoubtedly be the largest piece of furniture in the room and is often the first and most expensive purchase. But before you spend a lot of money on a desk, give some thought to the practical aspects of what you really need a desk to do.

> **Storage considerations**

No matter how sleek and fashionable an office may look furnished with a *table* (instead of a desk with drawers), if you plan to do real work in your office, get a desk *with drawers*. In most cases, a table will prove to be extremely impractical in the long run. You'll find that you need and want drawers to house supplies and important files conveniently. If your desk doesn't have drawers, your supplies and paperwork have no place to go when you're not working with them. Not only is this unsightly, you won't be as efficient and effective with unfinished tasks distracting you everywhere you look.

A desk should have at least one drawer deep enough to hold hanging files. Designate this drawer for a "tickler" file where you'll keep work-in-waiting. This kind of file gets its name because it tickles you—reminds you—of upcoming tasks based on the date you plan to work on them. You drop documents, notes, and reminders of all sorts into folders labeled for each day of the month. When you check them each day, they automatically trigger action and/or review when needed, relieving you of the need to think about them otherwise. Since this is a file you'll refer to constantly, it should be close at hand and separated from all other files.

A second file drawer, if the desk has two, can be used for documents you refer to regularly. These might be priority projects, current customers, or administrative and financial records. To make it easy to add new files when necessary, keep a few extra hanging files and folders there.

Shallow desk drawers are ideal for frequently used office supplies. Use drawer organizers to keep things like note pads, paper clips, pens and markers from ending up in a jumble.

If you already have a table instead of a desk, you can get a rolling cabinet with file and supply drawers that you can keep alongside you while you work. At the end of the day when you close up shop you can move it elsewhere.

> **Computer considerations**

So much work is done on computers these days there are new issues to keep in mind when choosing a desk. While you'll want a traditional thirty-inch high surface for *handwritten* work; for computer work you may want something different. If your monitor is at that height and you wear bifocal eyeglasses you'll have

25

difficulty seeing clearly without tilting your head back to get the proper angle. And if you regularly use a laptop as your primary computer, the keyboard will be at the wrong height if you place it on a traditional desk. You'll have to hunch up your shoulders to type which will give you major neck and shoulder problems before long.

If you're in either of these situations, look for a piece of furniture that's approximately twenty-five inches high—the traditional height for keyboard trays. It should be deep enough to accommodate a monitor and keyboard, or your laptop. At this height you can hold your head at a normal angle and type in an ergonomic position with your forearms parallel to the floor. You may be able to find a thirty- inch high desk that has a full-width keyboard shelf at twenty-five inches, or you may decide to attach an aftermarket pullout keyboard tray. If you can't find the perfect setup, you may have to place your monitor on a separate twenty-five-inch high piece of furniture right next to your desk/keyboard tray.

Work Table

If you often need space to spread out paperwork, assemble packets, or the like, consider a separate work table that you can leave undisturbed for as long as you need. This will help keep your work in your office instead of spread out on the dining room table where anything can happen!

Desk chair

When you're working from home, you'll probably sit at least couple of hours per day at your desk and/or in the front of a computer, so invest in a good chair or your back and shoulders will pay an ergonomic price. Get a chair that's comfortable to sit on and is adjustable in height so your thighs are parallel to the floor when your feet are flat and your arms are in the proper position for prolonged computer work—also parallel to the floor.

Here are a few recommendations for your desk chair:

> Choose one that swivels and has casters so you can move freely between desk, computer, and files.

> Look for supportive arms to reduce fatigue if you do extensive computer work.

> Invest in a floor mat that will make it easy to move around and will protect your floor. If your floor is carpeted, get one with teeth on the bottom so it's raised a bit above the carpet pile and won't mash it down. If your office has a hardwood floor, a mat that's smooth underneath will protect the floor from scratches.

Telephone

To project a professional image you'll definitely need a phone number that is *exclusively* for your business. When a client calls, it's neither professional nor cute if a child answers the phone. It's confusing even for an adult to answer if he or she isn't familiar with the details of your projects.

Rather than adding a second line to your home phone, consider using a cell phone as your business phone. Even better, make it a smartphone so you'll have your e-mail, contact list, to-do list, and calendar with you at all times. Your phone then becomes a portable office, making it convenient to do business anywhere. Here are some of the many advantages:

1. Because you aren't tied to a home phone and computer, you're free to leave your home for business meetings, family activities, personal errands, etc., without missing important messages. You still present the same professional image to your customers you would if you were at home in your office.

2. Much of the time you'll be able to answer the phone yourself and when you can't, digital voicemail will take the message. Callers will hear *your* voice, so they'll know they've reached the right number. They'll hear the kind of professional greeting they expect and not something listing options to reach various members of the family.

3. You'll be surprised how often *you* will get the job simply because you answered the phone when your competitors didn't.

4. You'll get an alert when you miss a call, so it won't take you all day to get messages when you're out. You'll be able to return calls quickly and address problems before they become acute. You'd be amazed what a difference this makes to customers who have become accustomed to and irritated by lazy customer service!

5. Since you always have your calendar with you, you can make appointments on the spot without fear of double-booking. You'll be seen as organized and efficient.

6. No matter where you are, when you find yourself with an unexpected snippet of free time you can make a few calls or complete something on your to-do list.

Computer and accessories

A computer is so central to business productivity that by the time you're working from home, you undoubtedly have a good idea of the technical specifications you need along those lines. So I'm not going to spend time discussing that. However, computers and their accessories are notorious for creating clutter, so I will take a few moments to suggest ways you can keep that under control.

Equipment like routers, cable modems, external hard drives, etc., shouldn't be on your desk. Your desk should be a *work* space that's free of distractions and visual clutter. Place these items somewhere else where their cords won't obstruct your desk drawers or other equipment. And label the cords at the plug ends so you can identify what you're about to unplug when you need to remove, replace, or rearrange equipment. Along those lines, I recommend that you keep instruction manuals close to the equipment they're for, so when you have a question or problem, you can find the information quickly.

Speaking of replacing equipment, when you do, opt for models with wireless connectivity in order to minimize cord clutter. In the meantime, if you can't stand the inevitable mess of tangled cords, there are all kinds of clips, straps, and covers at your office supply store to corral and conceal them.

Even if your office has plenty of electrical outlets, you'll probably need a power strip to accommodate all the equipment you acquire. Look for one with widely spaced or adjustable outlets to accommodate transformers or you'll end up with lots of unusable outlets.

Printer/all-in-one multifunction machine

Every business needs a printer, and unless you need specialty equipment for some reason, an inkjet all-in-one printer-fax-copier-scanner will be extremely convenient and space-saving. When you need a quick copy of something it's such a waste to have to go to a copy shop! Especially when it costs so little to have a copier right at your fingertips. And it's surprisingly convenient to be able to send and receive faxes, too. While an e-fax can be useful, not everything you want to fax will have been generated on your computer. Having a separate fax number also conveys that you are a "real" business.

But the most compelling reason to have a scanner is to minimize the paper you need to physically keep up with. Documents you'll refer to regularly or will want to share with others belong scanned into your computer where they're always easy to find. If you anticipate doing a *lot* of scanning, however, you'll find one of these combo machines to be too slow. Consider getting a high-speed desktop scanner that has an automatic feeder for multiple pages, or look into a scanning service that will do it all for you and return a CD you can store or download into your computer.

Document storage

> **Traditional file cabinets**

As your business grows, you'll accumulate documents that need to be stored. One of the *major* causes of paper clutter in an office is that there isn't adequate, convenient storage for paper documents. Accordion files or folders propped up on bookshelves will be clumsy, unstable and inconvenient; plan to get a good quality file cabinet or two. They're available in a variety of styles, finishes and configurations to fit your personal preferences and storage needs. If you're watching your budget, try Craigslist or a used office furniture outlet. It's more important that the drawers pull out smoothly when they're filled with papers than if your cabinet has a scratch or two. Two-drawer file cabinets often work best in a home office since you can reach the drawers while seated and they provide a place to keep books or a printer. They also double as room dividers.

> **Literature sorters**

Some people worry that if they put papers away in a drawer, they'll forget about them. If this is your concern, here's an unconventional idea you might like. Buy a literature or mail sorter—the kind with multiple cubbyholes—that you can use to keep papers together and organized, yet visible. You'd label the sections as you would with hanging files and file papers in them the same way. However, the papers in them would be horizontal rather than vertical.

Other storage

Businesses have other things to store besides paper. You undoubtedly have miscellaneous gear, books, and possibly product inventory, depending on the nature of your business. Group the things you need to store into categories to see just how much space you'll need. Decide what type of storage (bookcases, drawers, bins, shelves, etc.) will allow you to fit the storage you need into the space you have.

After you've done this planning, evaluate if what you have on hand will do the job. *Then*, visit your favorite discount, office supply, hardware, and specialty stores to fill in. Keep an open mind about where you look and exactly what you're looking for, because you may find something that's just perfect in a store you don't expect. When you spot something that appeals to you *and* fits your needs, grab it!

> **Miscellaneous Office Gear**

If you're short on drawer storage for small items, an over-the-door shoe pocket organizer can be a practical substitute. Get one with clear pockets, and you'll never lose sight of your back-up supply of paper clips, staples, or rubber bands again. This is also a good place for USB drives, extra batteries, pens, business cards, note pads, index cards, AC adapters, charger cords, and other bits of potential clutter. Label these last items so you can match them with the proper pieces of equipment.

> **Books**

If you have books you use for business, the most straightforward place to store them is in a bookcase. However, if you've been carting old books around for years without using them, reevaluate their usefulness. Some people find it almost impossible to part with books, even old textbooks they know they'll never open again, simply because they revere the knowledge they represent. If you feel that way, but really have no need for them to be in your office, store them elsewhere in your home. Be judicious, however; your dictionary and thesaurus might be more useful in your office.

A bookcase is also a good place for binders, magazine files, and software CDs. Office supply stores offer lots of options for keeping these items handy, yet organized. Once you have gathered together all the items that you want to keep in the bookcase, you'll be able to tell how large a bookcase you need. It's a good idea to get something a bit larger than your current needs to allow room for additions; in the meantime you can add photos, awards and decorative items to personalize your office.

⟩ Office Tools

Somewhere between the categories of office *supplies* and office *equipment* lies the category of office *tools*. Consider if any of these would be useful in your business:

⟩ Label maker to make files and supply areas look neat and professional

⟩ Timer to remind you to switch tasks or take a break now and then

⟩ Analog clock, whose moving hands show the passage of time, to increase your time awareness

⟩ Paper cutter for trimming photos and documents to size

> Three-hole punch if you assemble items into binders

> Plastic comb binding equipment if you assemble workbooks

> Heavy duty/electric stapler for thick documents

> Laminator for protecting photos, reference sheets, or other documents

> Power strips for office equipment

Shredder, recycle bin, and wastebasket

Another major reason that clutter accumulates in offices is that there isn't an easy way to get rid of it! Get some good-sized containers you can use for items that are on their way out of your office—a shredder for paper that includes confidential information, a recycle bin for nonconfidential paper that's recyclable, and a wastebasket for the rest. Keep them all near your desk so piles don't accumulate.

You may be dismayed to find that a good shredder will cost upwards of one hundred fifty dollars. But even a modest amount of shredding will overpower a "light duty" shredder costing less. Light duty shredders are prone to clogs and jams if you feed more than a couple of sheets at a time, and the motors will overheat and shut down after a few minutes. If you get a robust shredder it's a one-time expense and you won't have to replace it.

Security experts recommend "crosscut" or "confetti cut" shredders over strip cutters since the shred they produce is beyond reconstruction. It's hard to believe, but there are criminals willing to spend hours pasting shred strips together to find out your personal information!

Reading chair

If your work involves quite a bit of reading, and you have room in your office, consider a comfortable chair with a good reading light. The thought of doing extensive reading at your desk probably isn't too inviting, but curling up in a cozy chair means it's more likely to get done. And some people like to work on a laptop that's actually on their lap—another good reason to have a chair, maybe one with an ottoman so you can stretch out a bit.

One of the great benefits of working from home is that you're able to make your own choices about locating, setting up, and equipping your office. You can furnish it in a way that pleases *you*. You can choose paper or digital filing. You can do just about anything you want, as long as it works. You don't have to accept what someone else thinks you should have. The two most important considerations about your office are that you like it and that it helps you work effectively. It's *your* office, after all, so it must be right for *you*.

Get your office organized

If you're starting from scratch

Many newer homes already include a home office workspace, "bonus," or "unassigned" area that's an obvious choice for your home office. However, if your home doesn't have such a space and you're setting up a home office for the first time, here are a few things to think about.

1. **What spaces in the home could be converted?**

> Unused dining room or formal living room

> Guest bedroom

> Former bedroom of a child now living elsewhere

> Porch that could be enclosed

> Garage

> Attic

> Basement

> Dormer window

> Separate building on the property

2. How should you arrange the room?

> **Place the desk and chair first**

You'll want a desk that's deep enough to hold a desktop organizer for current projects and a few desk accessories like a lamp, clock, etc., and still leave you plenty of workspace. It should be long enough to provide adequate work space for paperwork with room on the sides for whatever files you may need at the moment. Personally, I think it should have drawers to house files and supplies that are used on a daily basis.

Usually it's a good idea to avoid having the desk front up against a wall. You'll use up most of the wall space and may feel limited or restricted because there's no open space in front of you. It's better to have the desk perpendicular to the wall.

A convenient layout to visualize is a U-shape: the desk being the front leg of the U, a side table (furniture manufacturers call it a "return") as the bottom of the U, and a credenza/lateral file cabinet of desk height as the back leg. These three pieces will enclose the area where you sit, so the desk and credenza/file cabinet need to be far enough apart to allow you access without being cramped.

Don't be tempted to skimp on a chair. Get one that's comfortable, supportive, adjustable, and on wheels. If possible, ask to buy it "on approval" and use it regularly for a couple of weeks. If you don't love it, take it back and try another that doesn't have whatever shortcomings you've discovered.

> **Group other major pieces according to their function**

Computer work

These days, most people do more work on their computer than they do manually at their desk. Often the side table—the return—is a good spot for your computer. Make sure it's large enough to hold a few papers or files you may be working with.

Ergonomically, it should have a keyboard tray at elbow height so that your shoulders don't have to hunch up to type as they would if the keyboard were at desk height. If your keyboard is at the wrong height it won't be long before you have major problems with your neck and shoulders! *Don't* put your computer on your desk unless your desk is very large and has a keyboard tray.

Filing

Place the file cabinets for everyday working files within easy reach. Two-drawer, lateral file cabinets are usually the most convenient format. You can swivel in your chair to file or retrieve papers and they provide another work surface. This is often a good spot for the printer and other office equipment.

Rarely used or archived files can be stored anywhere in the office, elsewhere in the home, or even scanned onto CDs.

When you're furnishing your office get more file drawer space than you think you'll need. Lack of sufficient file space is the single greatest reason for clutter in home offices!

Reference material

Some material you refer to will need to be stored someplace else besides a file cabinet because it's in some format other than paper. Place it according to how frequently you use it. If your reference material is in binders that you consult all the time, consider keeping them on top of the file cabinets, within easy reach. If you have a large number of books that you reference only occasionally, a bookshelf across the room is a better choice.

Other furnishings

Depending on the remaining space and the specific nature of your work, you may wish to add supply cabinets and/or a comfortable chair with a good reading light.

3. Is the infrastructure adequate?

> If the furniture arrangement doesn't match the number and location of electrical outlets, you'll probably want an electrician to make some changes. If you live in an older home, have the electrician ensure that your electrical set-up is capable of handling the demands of all the equipment you'll have. Same thing for reliable telephone and Internet connections.

> If you're thinking of converting a porch, garage, attic, basement, or out-building, consider what it will take to make it a comfortable working environment. You're likely to need some major heating, cooling, lighting, insulation, and/or electrical work.

> Restrain yourself from committing to built-in cabinetry in the beginning! After you actually work in your office for a year or two, you may very well decide the arrangement isn't quite right, in which case you'll want to make changes. Built-in cabinetry makes that an expensive proposition.

If You're Starting with a Mess

Sometimes you find yourself facing a situation that needs a total makeover to become an office you want to work in. Maybe the room that's to be your office used to be something else. Or perhaps you got so overwhelmed somewhere along the line that you just gave up trying to keep your office organized. This section will walk you through the steps to de-clutter and reconstruct your office. If you've got a totally unmanageable office and are ready to do a complete makeover, keep reading!

By the way, the task before you is not as uncommon as you might think! When people first set up their offices, it's hard to know how their businesses will evolve. As time goes by, they discover that what they *have* isn't exactly what they *need*, but they make do and work around and patch together until their workspaces are no longer workable! But once they have a better idea of what they need, they fix it. And so can you.

Why bother?

When your workspace is a disaster area, you can't work properly. There's a connection between your physical surroundings and your state of mind. When you're sitting on a peaceful beach watching the waves and the listening to the sounds of rustling palm trees, your mind is calm. When you're sitting in a traffic jam, listening to honking horns and idling engines, your mind is on edge. When you're trying to do serious work at home, your mind should be free of irritations, distractions, and annoyances so you can focus and work in peace.

If possible, I recommend that you pick a long holiday weekend or some other time when business is likely to be light so that you can plow through the mess and get it straightened out. While it's possible to do a complete overhaul in an hour or two here and there over several weeks, taking a day or two of uninterrupted time will be easier. Either way, the results will be well worth it! Once you're organized, vow to keep it that way so you don't have to do it again!

Get ready to work

You'll need cardboard boxes to sort things into. The best ones I've found are at Office Depot. They're called Quick Set-up Storage Boxes; get two or three four-packs. (You can return any you don't use, and once you've finished this project you'll find you can reuse them for lots of other things.) They're inexpensive and the dimensions fit hanging files, both letter and legal size. Plus, they have handles so you can move them and lids so you can stack them. Label the boxes Keep, Repair, Donate, Belongs Elsewhere (separate box for each room), Give To (separate box for each person), Shred, and Discard.

1. **Clear the surfaces of clutter**

> Start with the clutter on the floor, on the desk, chairs, and any other surfaces. Tackling this job first will pay off quickly because the improvement will be highly visible and will motivate you to continue organizing the entire office.

> Handle each item once and make a decision about which box it goes into. Experts have found that clutter is often the result of deferred decisions, so do the best you can to make quick decisions as you go. Resist the temptation to look through notebooks, magazines, and other items that could distract you from getting this done quickly. When you fill a box, move it out of the room and start another with the same label. Later, you'll revisit each box to go through the contents, but for now, just clear the decks.

> As you're sorting, be realistic about items that have gone unrepaired for years, articles that have gone unread for years, etc. Your goal here is to make your life easier, not to create more lists of things you need to do. If you're not certain you'll take action, place the items in the Discard box.

> When a lot of the clutter is paper, sometimes these decisions are not quite so easy. You may want to check the specific checklists in the *Process Paper Promptly* section to help you decide which papers to keep. At this stage, keep the paper if you're not sure whether you'll need it or not.

2. Clear the drawers, shelves, and cabinets to make room

> Clear out the shelves, cabinets, and drawers next so that you can create room for the items that haven't previously had a home. Remove whatever's broken, dirty, outdated, or no longer used. Continue sorting items into the same boxes as above, saving the papers until last.

> When tackling the file drawers, skim through each file to see if there are documents that are obvious-

ly outdated and can be discarded or shredded. If you're not sure, leave them in the file for the time being. If necessary, look at each piece of paper to determine if you need to keep it.

> If the files haven't been tended to in a long while, there may be so much unnecessary paper that the job turns out to be easier than you thought it would be. Before you start throwing things out, however, make sure you have established a record retention policy (consult your accountant and attorney) so you'll know what should be archived or destroyed.

3. Distribute the boxes you've sorted

> Throw out the Discard boxes (recycle the recyclables first), distribute the Belongs Elsewhere boxes to their respective locations, present the Give To boxes to their beneficiaries, and donate the Donate boxes to your favorite causes. Shred the paper that needs shredding or take it to a shredding service (some office supply stores offer low-cost shredding services for relatively small quantities).

> Take another look at the items in the Repair box to make sure they're worth repairing and/or will actually be used and put them in the car. That way you'll have them with you when you are near the appropriate repair shop.

Now you have only the items in the Keep boxes to deal with! Place items from the Keep box in appropriate locations based on how often you'll use them. Leave the papers for last.

4. Reconstruct the files

> Finally, deal with the paper. You'll need the same cardboard boxes you used for sorting, and a supply of hanging files with tabs and labels. If there are more files remaining in the file drawer than there is paper in the Keep boxes, re-build the files right in the drawer. If there are more papers in the boxes than remain in the file drawer, move the remaining files into the boxes and use them as temporary file drawers as you rebuild. The hanging files will hook over the edges of the boxes.

> Start reviewing the papers in the Keep boxes. As you identify the general category of each document, see if there's a file that seems to fit. If so, drop it in. Don't worry about being too precise or putting the individual documents in order. The goal here is to get each paper into *approximately* the right place so that you could find it again if you needed to. If there's no current file, create a hand-written label, slip it into a file tab, slip that into the slots in the hanging file, and drop the paper in. Place the tabs for all the hanging files in a straight line. This makes it easy to add files without disrupting a pattern of staggered tabs. Choose a location (left or right) for the tabs that will be easiest to see when the file cabinet drawer is opened.

> Keep the label categories fairly broad at this point; this step is just a stop-gap measure designed to get the papers into some sort of order. Add new categories as they present themselves.

> If you discover items that need to be acted on, place them in a stack on your desk. Unless there is something critical that must be dealt with immediately, continue organizing your papers and pro-

cess the stack on your desk later as recommended in the *Process Paper Promptly* section.

> As you add hanging files, arrange them in whatever order makes sense to you. It may be by category—for example, all financial documents together and all client files together, alphabetically within category. Or you may prefer to arrange *all* the files alphabetically. It doesn't matter, so long as it makes it easier for you to find the proper file.

> This process will give you a reasonably functional set of files that you can work with until you have completely finished creating your new system. You will have recently looked at each piece of paper, so you will be familiar with what's in the boxes. You will have categorized them to the point where you will know what file to look in and will be able to find what you need fairly quickly.

> When you have the time, you can go back and create printed labels for your files so they look neat and professional. You may decide to choose different colored hanging files to visually differentiate different categories. Visit an office supply store to see all the latest ideas for making your files attractive and functional.

When you're though with this project you will feel a huge sense of relief and accomplishment! Take a photo of your newly organized office and post it somewhere to remind you to keep it that way. Take a few moments each day and you'll never have to do this again!

Keep your office organized

Keeping your organized office provides an efficient and effective working environment and assures the rest of your household that things are under control. If you keep your office organized and clutter-free you'll be more productive. If the office becomes the family's dumping grounds or the children's toy box, you won't. So if an item finds its way into your workspace that doesn't belong there, remove it.

One of the most common difficulties people have in trying to organize an office is the belief that everything they use and everything they're working on needs to be visible. It's true that everything you need should be readily accessible; however, if your desk is covered with stacks of stuff, where will you work?

Any workspace will become unruly if there are no rules! Let me suggest a few:

1. Provide a home for every item in your office

Decide a logical and convenient place (*not* on top of your desk) for every item that's important enough to be in your office. Just like items in other parts of the house, items in your office need a place to be when they're not in use. When your clothing isn't being worn, it's in the closet; when you're not eating off your plates, they're in the cabinet. If items in your office have no designated home, they can't be put away and will perpetually drift around as clutter.

Be sure to provide a home (usually a tray or basket) for the current day's incoming mail. Make it a priority to process every piece of mail that lands here before the next wave arrives. Once you get behind, it's no longer current and you could miss something you need to act on.

2. Put items back where they belong when you're finished with them

Perhaps the single most important change you can make to keep your office organized is to adopt the simple habit of returning things to their assigned places when you're through using them. It only takes a few moments and will save you hours of searching and anxiety later. Don't just put things *down*; put them *back*.

3. Keep similar items together so you can find things

Create broad mental categories for items in your office so that it's clear where new ones belong. For example, books would be together on the bookshelf; computer supplies would be kept near the computer. If the category becomes so large that it becomes muddled, sub-divide it. So, a category that begins as "office supplies" might be better off separated into areas for paper goods, pens, software CDs, permanent markers, note pads, etc., as your business grows.

4. Keep work-in-waiting off your desk until you're ready to work on it

One of the biggest causes of clutter is that work accumulates faster than you can attend to it. If there's no specific place designated for work to wait, it will sit in stacks on your desk until your desk is covered; then it will start piling up on the floor. I recommend having a tickler file, which I discuss fully in the section titled, *Put Paper in Its Place*.

5. Each day before you leave the office, get ready for the next day

Return items you've used to their homes, consult your planner calendar and tickler file to make sure you have what you need for the next day's work, place those things on your desk and go in peace to the other activities in your life.

6. Keep control of your space

One of the great advantages to working from home is that the number of people in your office is limited. That means that even when you can't find something, you know it's in your office somewhere—*if* no one else has been moving things around! So, for the sake of peace and harmony and avoiding family arguments, make it a rule that nobody but you adds, moves, or *re*moves anything in, or from, your office.

This means that unrelated mail is handled elsewhere, notes aren't dropped on your desk expecting you to notice them, and children don't play in your office unless you're with them. If someone goes in there to clean, they need to work around whatever "mess" they find, perhaps only emptying the shredder, recycling bin, and wastebasket. The truth is that others will be less tempted to "tidy up" in your office if you leave it in a relatively organized state most of the time.

It's only natural for your workspace to become a bit disorganized over time, as with any area of a home that people actually live in. But don't let that be an excuse for letting things go entirely. It only takes ten to fifteen minutes each day to maintain any system of organization once it's been established. The only thing that stands between you and long-term organization is motivation.

It's worthwhile to review your supplies, reference materials, and office tools from time to time. You may find things that no longer work or that you no longer use and can discard them or pass them on to someone else. Then you can reorganize your workspace around your current needs.

Opt for an off-site office

Even when you have a fully equipped home office that you love working in, there are times when you want or need to work someplace else.

> Your home office environment is disrupted, such as for painting, renovation, or houseguests

> You find that staying on task is difficult with household distractions and temptations

> You'd rather meet with a client in a traditional business environment instead of at your home

> You're holding a meeting for a number of people and need a conference room

> You have time between appointments during the day but not enough time to return home

> You feel isolated at home and miss working around other people

> You're on a business trip and are working in airports and hotels

If you find yourself in a situation similar to any of those above, or your work involves visiting clients and attending events away from your home office, it's convenient to create an office that's portable. With a little planning and technology, you can remain productive, professional and organized no matter where you are.

Set up a portable office

> **Use a smartphone as your business phone**

You can do business from anywhere and always appear professional. You'll always have your e-mail and calendar with you and can make appointments or address problems on the fly. Ideally, your phone calendar syncs wirelessly with your computer calendar so both are always up to date.

❯ Consider using a laptop as your primary computer

❯ You can have all your files with you all the time. You'll be prepared for anything.

❯ If you have time enough between appointments to do substantial work, you can use its larger keyboard rather than your phone's tiny one.

❯ If you want Internet access, choose a place with free Wi-Fi, get a broadband access card from your cellular service provider, or use your smartphone as a hot spot.

❯ Keep a duplicate power cord in the car to make life simpler.

❯ Use a laptop or netbook to access your primary computer

❯ Even if your desktop at home remains your primary computer, it's still convenient to have access to current files and a larger keyboard.

❯ If you work on several different devices (desktop at home; laptop and smartphone when you're out) keep your hard drive files automatically synced among all of them with Dropbox (Dropbox.com). A change you make on any of them is reflected on all of them! The *free* Dropbox account has no expiration date and 2GB of storage space—probably enough for most of your active files. If you need more, there's a paid version.

❯ You can access everything on your home desktop computer from your laptop via Go To My PC (GoToMyPC.com) or LogMeIn (LogMeIn.com). They both allow you to connect via any other computer with an Internet connection. In addition to their ongoing subscription plan, Go To My PC has an inexpensive month-to-month plan that allows you to pay for only the months you want it—ideal for short-term needs. LogMeIn has a paid version with full access to all features, and a free version that lets you do the basics, but you can't print.

With so many work-from-home professionals needing occasional off-site work space, there are now a number of places you can set up a portable office:

Coffee shop

Coffee shops have become the default off-site location of choice for many solopreneurs. They're plentiful, there's no cost, many include free Wi-Fi, coffee and snacks are readily available, and the ambience in most cases is casual and welcoming. There's a pleasant buzz of background activity that's a nice break from the silence of your lonely home office. It's easy to have informal client meetings because these are public locations and usually parking is available and free. What's not to like?

Well, they're so popular that sometimes you can't find a spot to sit. Electrical outlets are scarce and often taken by the time you get there. Tables are relatively small and you're expected to share close quarters; you can't spread out much without being inconsiderate. Despite the close quarters, some people conduct loud and lengthy cell phone conversations, imposing on everyone within earshot. And even though the managers welcome solo workers, they do expect you to be a paying customer—especially when the lunchtime crowds roll in.

If you're working, or thinking of working, in a coffee shop you should understand the unspoken rules of etiquette:

> Don't take up more space than you need. Choose the smallest table that's available, and be prepared to share.

> Arrive with your computer fully charged. When you run low, charge up and then unplug. This allows others to charge their batteries while you're working off yours.

> Bring an outlet splitter or an extension cord. You'll be popular with your coworkers.

> Be politely friendly to your neighbors. Smile and acknowledge them.

> Be considerate of others when using your cell phone and keep your voice low.

> Buy something to eat or drink every so often.

> While the atmosphere is friendly, remember it is a public place; equipment and personal belongings shouldn't be left unattended. Most people do ask a friendly neighbor to keep an eye on their laptop if they step away for a few moments, but it's not a bad idea to bring a laptop lock along.

Shared office center

If you would rather have a "business" address for your business than a residential address, you can have one by signing on with a company offering shared office suites, usually in a distinguished commercial building. These are fully furnished, professionally equipped, individual, ready-to-work offices that share administrative support, meeting rooms, technical facilities, and other business amenities.

These companies offer packages at a variety of price points for a variety of needs—access for a single day, for several days each month, or every day for brief or extended time periods. Services start at the "virtual office" end of the spectrum, which means a mailing address and a live person to answer the telephone while you work at home—and extend all the way to the "full service office," which includes a private office with 24/7 access that's exclusively yours. Use of meeting rooms and advanced technical facilities and support are usually part of the full-service packages.

If your business caters to upscale clients or executives with major companies who expect you to have an office similar to their own, these shared office centers are a turn-key solution without the hassle, expense, or commitment of a commercial lease. In addition to the lower costs, this kind of shared office space can relieve the isolation that solopreneurs often feel, and sometimes business referral relationships develop. Even if that doesn't happen, you still have people to socialize with at the proverbial water cooler.

Co-working space

If you're the sort of person who thrives in a collaborative and creative work environment you probably find it very difficult to work alone in your home office. You want people to talk with about ideas and projects you're working on. A work style called "co-working" has developed over the last few years and it's designed for people like you. It's especially popular with freelancers involved in technology or creative arts where interaction is a big plus.

Co-working spaces tend to be open rooms filled with rows of adjacent desks. People can work quietly or chat with others. You can rent a desk, conference room, or office, by the day, week, or month; Wi-Fi is usually included and often so is secretarial service. Co-working is usually much less expensive than shared office space.

Some solopreneurs make a co-working space their permanent headquarters. It's a way of working alone without being alone. Working independently, but together.

Your car

Here are some ideas if you want to work efficiently and effectively from your car:

❯ Keep a laptop in your car

If you have a small computer that you can keep in your car, you can use its larger keyboard rather than your phone's tiny one when you find yourself with time enough to do substantial work. This is a great use for an older model that's not powerful enough to be your primary computer, but still works.

❯ Convert your car's power supply

Rather than buying multiple separate auto adapters for your laptop, phone, and other electronic gear, buy a single DC to AC inverter/converter that plugs into the cigarette lighter and lets you use any low-voltage AC item. Many have two or more AC outlets and a USB port, plenty to keep your equipment up and running all day.

❯ Keep a notebook nearby

It's handy to have something to write on to quickly capture a phone number or make notes during a phone conversation. You can jot down any ideas or follow-ups that occur to you, too.

A phone log notebook is ideal for this, especially the kind that automatically makes a carbonless copy. That way, you can leave one copy in the notebook for your reference and take the other with you for action or follow-up.

❯ Mind your mileage

If you're keeping track of mileage for tax purposes, it's helpful to have a mileage log close at hand. Personally, I find it's easier to get mileage from Google Maps or MapQuest than to remember to check the odometer each trip. If your appointments are noted in your calendar you can always reconstruct your mileage and enter it into your accounting program or a log you keep at home.

〉 Work surface and storage

To store work-in-your-car supplies, there are now quite a few car organizers designed specifically for this purpose. If you keep customer files with you, look for one that has a slot they'll fit into. If you choose one without closed compartments, gather pens, pencils, and other basic desk supplies into a plastic bag so they don't become flying projectiles in the case of a sudden stop.

Some of these organizers are canvas constructions that loop over the passenger headrest and lie against the back of the passenger seat. If you have a passenger, you just swing it around to the back. Some are open boxes with multiple compartments and rest on the passenger seat itself. You can place a flat surface over them to use as a work surface.

Some are a lot more substantial, taking up the entire passenger seat and meant to be more or less a permanent fixture. They have non-skid work surfaces, pull-out writing desks, room for dozens of hanging files and large storage areas underneath for keeping a laptop and other items out of sight. They can be moved, but it's a bit of work since they're strapped in with the seat belt. These are for cars that aren't doing double duty as family transportation.

› Create a "back and forth" carrier

Every day there will be things you need to transport between your house and your car. Some, like keys, will make daily round trips; others will just be going one way. Find a container you can use to transfer these items—something that's large enough to accommodate most of them, easy to carry, and stable enough that it won't lose its contents in transit. You'll then have a specific place to put things you want to take with you and will be much less likely to forget something.

An automobile office is like your office at home. It should make your work easier and more convenient. However, your car is out in public, so be aware that to some extent, it's a reflection of you and your methods. Keep it organized and presentable.

On the road

When you're going to be on the road for days at a time, make things easy on yourself:

› Keep it together

Create both a physical folder and a computer folder for each upcoming trip. Save flight confirmations, hotel and car reservations, notes about upcoming meetings, agendas, maps, and any other relevant information in whichever folder is appropriate. Add information about restaurants, local attractions, and other potential activities if you'll have downtime during the trip.

› Pack purposefully

If you travel with any frequency, create a standard packing list. Outfit a travel bag with all your essentials, and replenish them after each trip while their status is still fresh in your mind. Include a duplicate set of power cords, chargers, a flash drive, and basic office supplies, so you won't find yourself without some piece of critical equipment. Make it a habit to pack items in the same place every trip, so you can easily find them.

Determine a few sets of basic clothing that will look presentable even after a day of wear or being flattened in a suitcase and will be suitable for almost any occasion. Make this your standard travel wardrobe. Unless you see the same people every week, no one will notice that your wardrobe doesn't have much variety.

If you pack this way you can grab a bag on short notice, confident that you won't have forgotten anything. The goal is to save yourself time and trouble by not having to think your way through every packing operation as if it were the first time.

> **Expect the unexpected**

Be prepared for your checked luggage to go off on its own adventure. Before you turn it over to the airlines take a couple of photos, print them out, and keep them with you. If your bag goes astray, you can hand one to the airline representative—much easier than trying to describe your bag, especially if it looks like every other black bag. It's even a good idea to add a brightly colored bag tag or other distinct item to your luggage so that you can spot it easily at the baggage claim.

While you want to dress comfortably during the trip, wear something you don't mind being seen in, just in case that's all you have to wear for a day or two! And of course, keep critical supplies and information with you in your carry-on.

Download a program such as GoToMyPC or LogMeIn onto your travel laptop so you can access your primary computer at home in case you discover you need some piece of information you don't have with you.

Copy any presentations, important files, and your contact list to a flash drive and safeguard it as you travel. This precaution can save the day if your laptop or phone is lost or stolen, your battery conks out, or some other techno-disaster strikes. At least you'll be able to get hold of people you're scheduled to see and can run your presentation off someone else's computer if necessary.

> **Don't overpack**

When traveling most people over-pack their work, just as they over-pack their clothing. When you're planning a trip, think about the specific blocks of time you'll have available to work. How much can you do waiting at the airport, in a couple of hours on the plane, in your hotel room, and between appointments? Choose specific tasks you can accomplish during each of those time blocks and take with you only the information you'll need for those tasks. There's no point in dragging around more work than you can reasonably complete.

If there's general informational reading you need to do, this may be a good time to do it. When you're finished, you can leave it behind, making your return trip a little lighter or making room for new material you'll be bringing back.

> **Round up receipts**

Business travel involves lots of paper. When you're busy and on the go it can be a challenge to keep up with it all. Get in the habit of transferring all receipts, business cards, and other bits of important information at the end of each day to a single large envelope that you have marked in some obvious way. As you accumulate receipts and business cards add a quick note on each to remind you of the details and any colleagues who were present. Otherwise, you'll have a hard time reconstructing details for tax purposes.

One way to keep up is to snap photos of your receipts and business cards with a program like Evernote (Evernote.com), creating files on your smartphone. You might also consider taking along a portable scanner. Small and light, they scan receipts, business cards, and other documents, categorizing the information automatically so you can export it to standard accounting or contact database programs when you get home.

Don't forget to record expenses for which you don't get a receipt. Enter them in your planner/calendar or your smartphone.

> **Wrap up and follow up**

When you return home:

> As you unpack, update your packing list for the next trip. Add anything to the list that you forgot this time and delete things you took that you found you could do without.

> Replenish consumables and repack your regular travel inventory.

> Go through every bag and folder you took with you to capture any stray receipts, business cards, and notes you may have overlooked.

> Record all receipts and statements in your accounting program. Enter new contacts into your database.

> Schedule times in your planner/calendar to follow up on phone calls, e-mails and snail mail items that need attention.

> Schedule follow-up actions with new contacts.

Put Paper in Its Place

"I am not disorganized—I know *exactly* where everything is! The newer stuff is on top and the older stuff is on the bottom."

You could describe the above system for paper management as "inversely vertically chronological." Totally ineffective, but giving anything a fancy name makes it sound like a real system!

*E*ven with the prevalence of electronic information, paper is still important, and if you're not organized, it can take over your office until there's clutter everywhere. Piles of paper will keep you from being able to think clearly, prioritize, or stay on task since everywhere you look you'll be reminded of something else you need to do.

The easiest way to control paper is to throw away (or recycle) as much as you can, as soon as you can. The more excess paper in your office, the more difficult it is to find the few important documents you really need. So here are a few suggestions to keep paper under control.

Prevent paper pileup

Paper you never receive is paper you don't have to process, sort, file, etc. Keep unnecessary paper out of your life by choosing automatic deductions and online bill payment whenever possible. Unsubscribe from magazines you no longer find worthwhile. Have your name removed from direct marketing mailing lists.

Purge the superfluous

Don't automatically keep everything that arrives in your mailbox. When you process your mail, immediately discard anything that doesn't need action, is of no interest to you, or doesn't need to be saved for a specific purpose. Open your mail over your shredder and immediately shred credit card offers and other solicitations that could lead to identity theft.

Direct personal letters and bills immediately to their designated locations where they won't be forgotten. Put magazines, newsletters, etc., wherever it is you do leisure reading.

Resist the thought that you can't spare five minutes to look at your mail each day. Processing your mail daily helps keep you organized, reduces clutter, and eliminates the chance you'll overlook something important or time-sensitive.

Go Paperless

People have been talking about the "paperless office" since the mid-seventies, and some expected it to happen within twenty years. Needless to say, it still hasn't happened! That's not to say that paper use hasn't decreased. It has, but very slowly. In reality, it's a bit more difficult than people imagined.

Why don't more businesses cut out paper completely and go digital?

> Paper is familiar; it's a habit.

> Everyone who works with computers knows it's possible they'll crash, erasing critical data. Hackers may break in, compromising systems and stealing confidential information. Large companies are tempting targets.

> It takes time and effort to religiously back up data so that if the computer does crash, you can recover. There's *no* fail safe protection from malicious cyber-intruders.

> In larger companies it's too difficult to coordinate interdepartmental training and security safeguards to keep everyone on the same page when multiple employees have access to company data.

> It takes more time up front to scan and file documents on a computer than to drop them in a file drawer.

> Expensive scanning equipment is required and the faster and more convenient it is, the more expensive it is.

In a small business you run from home, you may not be able to go completely paperless , but you can go paper-*less*! There are plenty of reasons you'd want to:

1. Paper takes space to store and money to buy.

2. Ink costs money and cartridges invariably run out when you're in a rush.

3. It takes time to retrieve a document even if your files are cleaned out and well organized. And whose files are really cleaned out and well organized?

4. Paper is easy to misplace or discard mistakenly. It's vulnerable to water and fire.

So it's worth a reasonable amount of money, time, and effort to gain convenience and space by generating and storing most of your work on your computer. You can:

> Copy or sync files between computers and/or your smartphone so you have access to important information no matter where you are.

> Easily share digital files with colleagues and clients.

> Quickly find documents when you want to refer to them.

> Cut and paste from one document to another, saving yourself an enormous amount of time.

> Create your own reference library that takes up no physical space by scanning articles you want to read or think you'll need to refer to in the future. In paper files, they can get lost or forgotten before you ever get around to reading them. You can even import them into your e-reader if you save them as PDFs, so while you're waiting for a meeting or a delayed flight, you can get caught up!

> Store vast quantities of information in no space at no additional cost.

If you want to use digital more and paper less, here are some ideas.

1. Don't print out e-mails or other documents that come to you via your computer. Create folders on your computer with labels that match your paper files and leave those documents on your computer.

2. Have your bills and statements delivered electronically.

3. Use online banking and bill-paying. Send e-checks instead of paper checks.

4. Get a scanner. Scanning documents and storing them electronically will dramatically reduce your paper clutter. There's a wide choice in scanning equipment, so choose something that suits your business lifestyle. Think about whether you'll use the scanner primarily to store documents just as they are, or if you'll want to be able to edit what you scan. Virtually all good-quality scanners offer optical character recognition (OCR), but some are more sophisticated and accurate than others. However, even a good quality scanner won't read everything perfectly, so you'll still need to proofread.

Portable scanner

If you travel frequently and want to scan paperwork as you go, a portable scanner is perfect. These devices can take care of a few days' receipts, meeting hand-outs and business cards. Be sure that if the scanner uses proprietary software it will allow you export the receipts and business cards into a commonly used program like Microsoft Excel and the documents into PDF or Microsoft Word format. The cost for these little scanners is generally in the range of one to two hundred dollars.

All-in-one printer/scanner/fax/copier

If you travel infrequently and your scanning needs aren't heavy, this is a very cost-effective and space-efficient way to go. You'll probably be getting an inkjet printer anyway unless you're in the graphic arts and need a top-quality *laser* printer. So get one of these multi-function units and you'll have the extra features at very little extra cost. Sliding up the price scale a bit, you can get one that does "duplex" scanning—extremely useful if the documents you need to scan are printed on both sides. Also, think about choosing a model that connects wirelessly to make it easier to arrange your office and keep cord clutter under control.

Even though you may not anticipate doing much scanning, do get a model that includes an automatic document feeder so you don't have to place each page individually on the glass. Having to do that will be so tedious that you probably won't do much scanning at all!

High-speed desktop scanner

If you anticipate doing a great deal of scanning, consider a stand-alone dedicated desktop scanner. These machines are expensive and will take up quite a bit of room, but they're built to make quick work of stacks of documents on a regular basis. Expect to pay five hundred dollars or more for a quality unit.

Scanning service

If you know you're not likely to do the scanning yourself, or if you have a backlog of documents you want scanned, an offsite scanning service may make sense for you.

Some services provide you with pre-paid envelopes you mail to them periodically; they return a CD that you can store as-is or download to your computer. You can have them return your documents if you want to keep the originals, or they'll shred them for you if you prefer. As an alternative, you might find a "document management" or "document imaging" company near you geographically, which eliminates the anxiety of sending off your documents to parts unknown through the mail. You can hand-deliver them to the company or if the volume is great enough they may come to pick them up.

By now you know that if you're going to rely on a computer for anything, you must have a good backup system! Back up *daily* to an external hard drive or a Web-based application. There are many online back-up services available, so investigate features, pricing, and ease of use. For most people, a process that hap-pens automatically will be more likely to be used than one that requires action on your part, no matter how good your intentions are.

Prevent paper pileup

It's smart to have a routine for processing mail and other paper promptly before it gets out of control.

> Install a mail station near the door where mail en-ters your house. This can be a shelf, a small table, or a spot on the kitchen counter, so it needn't take up much room, but it should have a sorter with sections for each person and a *separate* one for your business.

> Process your mail daily to stay organized, avoid clut-ter, and minimize the chance you'll overlook some-thing important.

> Get the family in the habit of immediately throwing junk mail into the wastebasket and separating the rest of the mail into the sorter for each person to deal with.

> Keep a shredder and wastebasket/recycle bin nearby.

Process Paper Promptly

"Processing" paper means deciding what to do with it. If you don't make a decision about what to do with every piece of paper, clutter is the result. Therefore, it's important to have an easy process for making decisions. Use my two favorite checklists below to help you decide what to do with your paper.

The first, the "*A-SORT—Keep or Toss*" checklist, provides very specific criteria to decide which papers should be kept or tossed. The second, the "*5-D—Next Action*" checklist is for deciding the next action you should take with a given piece of paper. Using these two guidelines will make short work of processing paper, whether it's just arrived or has been in your files for a long time.

I. The "A-SORT—Keep or Toss" checklist

As you go through your papers, remember that you are doing "A SORT." Ask yourself the following questions to determine which papers to keep or toss.

> **A** Is there **ACTION** required of me? (If no, toss.)

If there's information you need to take note of or enter in your calendar/planner, do so first. For example, if it's an announcement about an event you won't be attending, toss it. If a contact has a new e-mail address change your records, then toss it.

> **S** Is there something **SPECIFIC** I will do with this within **SIX** months? (If no, toss.)

This will weed out items you might like to do *something* with *someday*, but will realistically never get around to.

> **O** Could I **OBTAIN** this information elsewhere if I needed it? (If yes, toss.)

If it's on the Internet, in someone else's files, or on your computer, you don't need a hard copy.

> **R** Is the information **RECENT** enough to still be **RELEVANT**? (If no, toss.)

If it's old and outdated, don't keep it. You can find up-to-the-minute information on almost anything on the Internet. Of course, we're talking about information here, not cherished family photos and documents—keep those!

> **T** Are there **TAX**, legal, or financial reasons to keep this? (If no, toss.)

Ask your accountants, lawyers, and financial advisers for their recommended retention schedules, but once again, if they can provide copies of your records when you need them, you don't really have to keep duplicates.

2. The "5-D – Next Action" checklist

As you encounter each piece of paper, you need to make a decision about the next action that is required There are a limited number of choices open to you— and they're easy to remember, because they all begin with the letter **D**.

> **D**iscard it (according to the A-SORT checklist above)

> **D**elegate it or **D**irect it to someone else if you can (write a note with directions if necessary)

> **D**o it immediately (if it will take two minutes or less)

> **D**efer action until later (BUT, decide *what* action you will take and *when*; then enter it on your cal-

endar/planner for that date and place in the cor-
responding tickler file folder)

> **D**rop it in a file (only if you *really need* to keep it
based on the A-SORT checklist above)

Keep Top Priorities on Top

Despite what the "clean desk" advocates say, some papers absolutely *do* belong on top of your desk all the time.
Files you access every day should be in your line of sight
and at your fingertips. This includes current projects you're
actively working on every day, issues that are on hold until you hear back from someone else, and meetings that
are coming up in the immediate future. You should always
know exactly where these files are and be able to grab them
at a moment's notice.

It's best to keep these where you can see them, on top
of your desk, *standing on edge* in some sort of upright hold-
er. Upright organizers are ideal for keeping these top priority files out of your way yet still instantly available. "Riser" or
"step" files, designed so that each file folder is slightly higher
than the one in front of it, make their labels easy to see. In
contrast, once you add something new to a horizontal tray,
whatever's underneath disappears.

File and Find Documents Fast

The only reason to file papers is to give them a place to
be until you need them again. So before you file *anything*,
run it past the "A SORT—Keep or Toss" checklist to decide
if you need to keep it at all! Studies consistently show that
80 percent of papers filed are *never referred to again!* Don't
spend time creating an elaborate system or automatically
file everything that comes your way. A good filing system
should take you very little time to *file* or *find* documents.

There's no one best filing system. The best system *for you*
will depend on what kinds of documents you file and how

you'll think to search for them. Design your own system as you discover what works best for you. And what works best may be a *combination* of systems. Here are some ideas to get you thinking.

> **Don't make filing unpleasant**

Some people dread filing because they've let it go for so long that now there's a huge pile that's overwhelming. Sometimes it's because the file cabinet is jammed full and there's no room for new papers. Or the drawers scrape and stick when you try to pull them out. Or it's inconvenient because you have to cross the room or stand up to reach the right drawer. Many times, it's because the system is too complicated and it's not clear where papers should go. Files that are hard to use are files you don't want to use and probably won't use!

> **Buy a decent quality file cabinet**

It doesn't have to be new; it doesn't have to be fancy. But your file cabinet should be sturdy enough to hold the weight of a drawer full of paper. It shouldn't threaten to tip over when the top drawer is pulled out. It shouldn't have raw edges that scrape your knuckles when you're trying to file.

> **Use two-drawer lateral file cabinets**

Usually, a two-drawer lateral file cabinet, one that opens on the long side, is practical for a home office because the top can double as a work surface or can hold office equipment. A front-opening file gives you little accessible surface area for such uses. Also, lateral files are easier to work in than front opening files since you can roll your chair right up next to them and see a great many files at once. The space allowance required for them when they're open is also modest, making it easier to arrange office furniture.

〉 Use hanging files

Use hanging files that slide along a metal rail inside the file drawer. They're more convenient for active files than loose folders in a drawer with no internal structure. Some older file cabinets don't have built-in rails for holding hanging files; instead they have a metal sliding support that moves up from the back of the drawer to hold folders in place. These may be acceptable for archived files you don't need to access often, but you have to keep the folders compressed or they slump in the drawer and it's awkward to be moving the slide back and forth all the time.

If your cabinet doesn't have built-in rails, you can buy inexpensive wire frame inserts at office supply stores. Or if it once had rails or bars that have since disappeared, you can order replacements online.

〉 Don't overstuff the drawers

Keep your file drawers less than three-quarters full. There should be enough open space to get files in and out with ease. In my opinion, there's usually no need to use interior folders insider each hanging file; they just add bulk. An exception would be when you have sets of closely related documents that you want to keep separate but together in the same hanging file. For example, a file might be labeled "Public Relations," with separate interior folders for news releases you send out and articles published by others about you.

〉 Keep documents unencumbered

Don't put papers back into envelopes as you file them. That just makes it necessary to re-open the envelope to remind yourself of the contents. If you need the return address from the envelope, take a moment and add it to your database.

Remove paper clips; they fall off or get caught on other papers. Instead, staple papers that belong together. If an item is too large to fit flat in a file, fold it with the printed side facing *out*. This eliminates the need to remove and unfold it just to see what it is. Consider reducing outsized documents to letter size if your copier will do so and the document will still be legible.

〉 Label files clearly

For professional looking files, use a handheld label maker or a template for printed computer labels. Handwritten file labels can look messy, especially if some are in pencil, some in ink, some printed, and some scribbled.

To make file labels easy to read, most organizing experts today recommend inserting plastic tabs all in a straight line—left, center, or right. Many files become difficult to visually navigate when the tabs are randomly staggered. Systems that begin with the tabs in a regular staggered pattern become disorderly as soon as new files are introduced. With straight line tab placement, adding new files is seamless.

〉 Keep categories broad

Filing by category provides a logical structure for files because similar subjects are grouped together. If you choose a different color for each category, it's easy to see where they're located as soon as you open the file drawer. Aim for category labels broad enough that most new documents fit one of them. Create a new category when necessary but don't make them so specific that you create a new file for every new piece of paper.

For example, in most small businesses, there's no need to subdivide a category called "Legal" into permits, licenses, trademark registrations, etc. You just don't need to be that specific; one file is plenty. If it has to do with legal matters, drop it in; if you have to retrieve it later you can thumb through the file until you find the right document. On the other hand, a category called "Clients" wouldn't be specific enough. It would be impractical to put all your individual client folders into one hanging file; you'd want separate files for each one, probably arranged alphabetically. And you'd want them all to be the same color, so you know instantly that a file that's yellow, for example, is a client file.

Ideally, when adding a new document you'll place it in the *front* of the file, but I don't think it's a big problem if you don't. Files shouldn't be so thick that it takes more than a moment or two to find what you're looking for no matter where it is in the file. If files become too crowded, subcategorize or weed out outdated information.

> **Place files based on frequency of use**

Keep the files you use all the time in the most convenient location, just like you would with any other office tool. Keep the ones you use less frequently a bit farther away—perhaps across the room, and the ones you seldom use even farther away, maybe in a storage closet.

❯ File routine statements by month

Think how fast and easy filing would be if you simply dropped all bills from the current month into one file and were done with your filing! Though most of us learned to file by vendor—telephone bills together, credit card statements together, etc., it's far easier to file all the bills from January together, all the bills from February together, and so on. Filing by month might be a bit more trouble *if* you need to find a specific bill from the past, since you'd have to guess at approximate timing and might have to check a few different files. But most of the time, we never refer to past bills anyway, so the filing time you will *definitely* save up front more than offsets the time you *might* spend later on.

It's a good idea to keep two years of monthly files, rotating the current year's files to the back when the year ends and bringing last year's file forward. This is how the FreedomFiler (FreedomFiler.com) system works. As the bills come in for the new year, review what's in the file from two years ago, and if you no longer need it, shred it. If you do need it, you can move it to a permanent "category" file at that time. Not only is this technique fast and easy, it automatically keeps your files from becoming stuffed with outdated paper.

❯ Consider unconventional filing methods

❯ File by index

The Paper Tiger (ThePaperTiger.com) system is a totally different way to file that can solve the problem of where to file papers that belong to more than one category. It also eliminates the need to remember exactly where you filed something. With Paper Tiger, you create a file index on your

73

computer by assigning a number to each new file *and new file folder* in the order that it's created. Then you add as many key words as you need to be sure you can find it again. When you search on those key words a list of all files with those words will be brought up. You'll spot the one you want, and be able to find the folder immediately by its number alone.

> Use a literature sorter

There are some people who just are not going to use a file cabinet, no matter what. If you're one of them, consider using a literature sorter or mail sorter instead; your papers can be just as organized as they would in a file cabinet. The trick here would be to label the slots descriptively and arrange them in a way that you can find the one you're looking for. If you're constantly adding new categories this could be difficult; however, if your categories are few and well established this might be a solution.

> Use binders

Loose-leaf binders can be a good choice when for legal, financial, or reference purposes it is important to keep a complete set of documents in a particular order, in a semi-permanent format. If you're working with very active files, it can be time consuming to punch holes and find the proper spot in the binder every time you want to add a new page. However, a binder is easy to grab off a shelf if you need to take a large file with you someplace. Properly labeled page dividers make it easy to turn to the exact document you want, and papers are secured—they unlikely to fall out as they might from an open folder.

〉 File as you go

If you keep up with filing when it's not a huge chore, a well-designed file system can help you be more productive and less stressed. Your files will be easy to find because they'll be in one of only two places—in use on your desk or in their proper place.

Don't create "to-file" piles. When you have something in your hand that belongs in a file, place it there immediately. If you're already backlogged, set aside fifteen minutes a day to get caught up. Even if you hate filing, you can do it for a few minutes! If after fifteen minutes you can stand it, do another fifteen. If that's all you can bear, congratulate yourself, stop, and do it again tomorrow.

Stay on track with a tickler file

There will always be papers you need to act on, and when you can't get to them immediately they need a place to wait until you can. If you just leave them in stacks on your desk and elsewhere around your office something is practically guaranteed to fall through the cracks, and in the meantime you'll have a cluttered, disorganized office. Yet, you don't want to put them away somewhere and forget about them. The solution is to set up a tickler file to hold these papers, remind you, or "tickle" you about what you need to act on and present you with whatever paperwork you need to do it. Of course, for this file to work you need to review it *every single* day!

A tickler file is composed of folders labeled 1-31 for each day of the current month, and folders labeled January through December for the whole year. As you sort papers, you put them into the folders for the days of the *current* month, or the folder of the *future* month that you plan to work with them. At the beginning of each month, you take the papers from the new month and distribute them into the 1-31 folders on the day you will work with them. You coordinate the tickler file with your schedule by blocking time for the task in your planner/calendar on that same day.

If your workload is fairly light, you can use a tickler file in a book format you can keep on your desk. These can be found in most office supply stores or catalogs. If you have lots of paper to hold until later, use a tickler file that can handle the volume. Create one using hanging files in a nearby file drawer. Remember, you need to look at that tickler file *every day!*

You can use a tickler file to hold follow-up notes, travel itineraries, registration forms, meeting agendas, greeting cards, renewal notices, anything at all that you don't need to deal with right now but you want to appear at the right time in the future. The file keeps track of the physical paper so when the task shows up on your planner/calendar, the paper shows up, too. Once you get in the habit of using a tickler file, you'll never want to be without one.

Put business cards to work

Most small business owners have business cards cluttering up their desk drawers, in-boxes, and other spots around the office. If that's the case, they're not helping you or the people you got them from. The reason to collect business cards is to do business with those people. Just think of all the contacts you've made that you've never followed up on! What are you missing in terms of clients you could gain, services you could use, and referrals you could exchange! This is especially important if you own a small business. Unless you make contact information easy to use, you might as well throw the card away.

Get those cards organized! Go through your stacks and toss the cards of individuals or companies you no longer recognize. Put those that are worth keeping into some kind of order. One option is to store them in a physical system—plastic notebook pages, rotary files, card wallets, or the miniature file cabinets available in office supply stores. These systems have one major drawback, however. You must decide how you will arrange the cards—by *individual* name OR by *company* name. If you choose *individual* name, and you can only recall the *company* name, how will you find the card? And what if you travel to another city? How will you identify your contacts there? How do you identify all the contacts you have at one particular company? Or those you met at a specific event? And if you keep business cards in a physical file of any type, what happens when you're out of the office and don't have the file with you?

Create a database

Convert the cards into a searchable database, which will be far more functional. You can do this by entering the information manually into Outlook or some similar application, or do it more quickly and easily using a card scanner. These clever devices read business cards and automatically distribute the information into the proper fields in their software. You can imagine how many advantages there are to converting business cards into a database. You can:

1. Add personal notes to the records about to jog your memory in the future

2. Search for a contact if you remember *anything at all:* name OR company OR where you met OR what you talked about, etc.

3. Export the data to your phone so that you always have it with you, to use yourself or pass on to a colleague as a referral

4. Export the data to your e-mail contact list to make it easier to stay in touch

5. Easily update the records when phone numbers or addresses change, or when you want to add information

6. Avoid wasting time wading through dozens of cards hoping to spot the *one* you're looking for

However, as with any optical scan system, you'll need to proofread carefully to make sure the information was captured correctly and went into the right data fields. If you don't have the time to do this yourself, it's the perfect task for a virtual assistant or college student. A virtual assistant may even have a card scanner already. If you decide to buy a scanner, they're not terribly expensive and can be a great investment you'll use for years. Or take a look on eBay. There are always people upgrading to the latest gadget and selling their old one that still works perfectly.

In the future, take a moment while new contacts are fresh in your mind to note on their cards where you met them, what you talked about, and other information that will help you remember them. Enter them in your system, whatever it is, before the cards turn into clutter. There, you've made your office *look* better, *work* better, AND you've made it more likely you'll do business with your contacts!

Reduce your to-read stacks

Most people don't have time to read everything that looks interesting. While it's important to keep up with topics pertinent to your job, unless you have a strategy, you'll soon have an unmanageable stack. Be selective about what you read and how much you keep.

If there are trade journals or newspapers you read, find out if the publication has an online version you can subscribe to instead of hard copy. That will eliminate clutter and the pressure of accumulating unread magazines.

When a new issue comes out quickly skim the table of contents to see if it contains pertinent information. Keep in mind you don't have to remember *everything* in an article you spot, just the major points. Later, if you need to, you'll be able to find that article and more simply by searching the archives.

For that very reason, unless an article is unusually comprehensive or insightful, it's not worth filing for future reference. If you feel you simply MUST keep it, scan it into your computer and place it in a meaningfully labeled folder with other related topics. It's more likely you will remember you have it, and you'll see the related information, too.

> If you realize you rarely come across important information in a particular publication, cancel your subscription.

> When an online version isn't available, tear out just the articles you wish to read; don't keep the entire issue.

> If you already have a big stack of reading, discard anything that's more than three months old. Undoubtedly you can find more up-to-the-minute information on the Internet.

> Keep all your "to-read" items in a single folder that's easy to take with you when you anticipate having a few moments of waiting time. A few articles at a time will eventually clear the entire folder.

Conquer Computer Challenges

"A corned beef sandwich with fries for me and some Spam and cookies for my computer."

We spend lots of time on the care and feeding of our computers. We shouldn't fill them up with junk! That means keeping your computer files organized. If you don't, you'll waste time you likely can't spare.

Constrain computer clutter

For small businesses, our computers are the gateway to just about everything we send and receive. With so much information coming and going, they can become disorganized if they're not properly taken care of.

Some people were never taught how to file computer documents properly. All their documents wind up either on their desktop or in their My Documents folder by default— the digital equivalent of just dropping all your papers loose into a file cabinet! No wonder you can't find them.

If your computer files aren't very organized, a search tool like Google Desktop (Desktop.Google.com) can help you find whatever documents may be lost. This program searches your own hard drive like a browser searches the Internet. You simply enter the word or words you're looking for and it returns a list of documents containing them. It's a lifesaver when you're having trouble locating a file. And it's *free!* However, no search tool can match the ease of being able to go directly to the folder or file you want. The following tips will save you time and trouble when dealing with your computer files.

Match your computer files to your paper files

When you create new documents you *can* prevent them from disappearing into some unknown place inside your computer where you'll never find them again. The answer is to create a file structure that matches your paper files.

Once you have an efficient arrangement for your paper files, set up your computer files with the same categories and in the same order. With files coordinated this way, you'll find it much easier to locate what you're looking for.

It's easy to understand your computer's file structure if you use Windows Explorer. To access it go to Start > Programs > Accessories > Windows Explorer. (If you use a Mac, it's Finder > Your Name > Desktop, Documents, etc.)

1. Folders = major categories within file drawers

2. Sub-folders = individual hanging files

3. Files = individual documents within the files

Corral bookmarks or favorites into categories

It's easy to bookmark interesting websites thinking you'll revisit often, but soon you end up with an unmanageable list that's dozens long! Bookmark sites sparingly. It can often be faster to find something using a search engine than to hunt through a long list of unorganized bookmarks. Delete the ones you never use and categorize the rest so you can make sense of what you have.

Download to your desktop

When you're downloading new programs (.exe files) to your computer, always save them to your desktop unless the program specifies a different location. They'll be easier to find when you're ready to install them. When you're finished installing, you can drag them to a single folder on your desktop that you've created and labeled Misc Programs. This trick will clear your desktop, yet keep your programs handy in case you need to reinstall them.

Save space by scanning

An article you want to read, or think you'll want to refer to in the future, will take up space and can get lost if you print it out and file it in a physical file. By the time you're ready for it, you may not even remember that you saved it. But if you scan items into your computer and save them in logical files with meaningful names (so you or Google Desktop search can find them), you'll create a convenient reference library that takes up no physical space at all!

If you save articles as PDFs, you can even import them into your e-reader and catch up on your reading while you're waiting for a meeting or a delayed flight.

Keep current

Computer files get cluttered just as physical files do. Don't spend time continually reviewing long lists of old folders and files, looking for the handful you currently use on a regular basis. One click on the top of the "Date Modified" column in Windows Explorer will arrange your files by date so you can review and delete old files you'll never need again. If you're not sure you're ready to delete certain files, an easy way to de-clutter is to consolidate files. Create a few subfolders and label them by year, client, status, or whatever categories are logical for you. Just drag the files and drop them in. If you need them, they're there, but out of the way in the meantime.

Manage digital media

When you're running a business, you'll encounter all sorts of digital media:

Computer software

When you're upgrading to a new computer or reinstalling software after some failure, you may dread the search for product installation key codes. We know we should keep every piece of documentation for software we install, but sometimes we remove a CD from its original case to save space, and it's easy to lose track of the product key. So when you install software for the first time, take a permanent marker and write the product key right on the software CD. Then it's always right where you need it.

Audio

In addition to whatever music you store on your computer, you may find that you soon have a collection of recorded telesessions, meetings, motivational speakers, interviews, and audio books. And it's likely you won't be able to listen to all of them as soon as you'd like. Just like any other type of material, create folders to organize your audio library until you're ready to use it.

Regardless of the format, group files on similar topics together in the same computer folder and be sure to re-label these files in a way that their content will be apparent to you. When you're ready to listen, you can easily review your choices, whether you play the file directly from your computer or download it to a mobile device to keep you company on the road or at the gym.

Video

The popularity of video communication has exploded over the last few years since it's more engaging than audio alone, and it's notably search engine friendly. In addition to professionally produced DVDs, you'll end up with webinars, videos you shoot yourself, and an infinite variety of clips downloaded from the Internet.

I'd suggest placing these in the same folders as your audio files so that all the information on a given topic is together. Again, re-label if necessary to make the content clear to you.

Photos

Every small business accumulates a collection of photos that needs to be managed. We use photos to show products, to document before and after transformations, and to record events. We use them on websites, in promotional material, in online profiles, and to share with friends and colleagues. Storing digital photos on your computer saves space and time since you don't have to sort through physical photos when you're looking for something specific. But they do need to be organized in some way. Here are a few things to keep in mind:

> Eliminate the photos you know aren't good enough to use. You'll save space on your computer and it will be easier to spot the ones you want.

> Group similar photos into folders using labels that are specific enough you won't have to open the folder to remind yourself what's in there.

> If you purchase stock photos, include the source in their file name for future reference.

> Remember that you can duplicate photos to keep them in more than one folder. So, *all* your stock photos might be together in one folder called "Source iStockphoto" and *some* of them might *also* be in a folder called "People Working," which would include all photos of people on the job regardless of source.

E-books

E-books are well on their way to outselling books in hard copy. Often you'll download an e-book to your computer first, where it might find a permanent home, or you might transfer it to a more portable device—an e-reader, digital notebook, or smartphone. These files will usually be pre-labeled so it should be easy to find the title you're looking for. However, if you download a lot of e-books you might want to categorize them by genre.

Flash drives

USB drives, thumb drives, flash drives—whatever you call them you can't beat them for portability and ease of use. These little gadgets have huge capacities these days and aren't very expensive. You can copy all your most important files to take with you when you're traveling. You can use them for routine backup. You can transfer files between computers. You can store your passwords on them so you can login to password protected websites automatically on any computer.

Buy several of different shapes or colors and always use the same one for the same function. That way you'll know which one has which data on it.

Find what you've filed

Place your documents in the right place in the first place

Get in the habit of using File > Save As, then naming your document and placing it in a folder with other related information. Keep all related documents together, regardless of the program used to create them. For example, customer documents might include PowerPoint presentations, Excel spreadsheets, correspondence created in Word, digital photos in JPG, invoices in PDF, etc. They should all be together in a single folder under the customer's name. If you use the same first word (for example, the customer's name) in every related file they'll group themselves together when you sort alphabetically.

Name documents descriptively

When you name a document, use meaningful words you'll recognize months from now when you're looking for that document. Provide enough information to identify it so you don't have to open the file every time to remind yourself what it is. For example, don't name a document "Letter Sept 17;" call it "XYZ Company – Speaker Confirmation National Meeting." Also, don't add unnecessary information like the date since it's already shown alongside the file name.

As you're creating your computer file structure, create subfolders as necessary. Within one client folder you may want to keep invoices, photos, and correspondence in separate subfolders. Just as with paper files, if there are only a few documents in a folder and it's easy to spot the one you're looking for, leave them there. But once you accumulate a dozen or more documents, it's probably time for subfolders.

Relocate documents temporarily

If you're using certain documents regularly, as you might when working on a project, consider creating temporary desktop shortcuts to access them quickly. When you're finished, delete the shortcuts and the files will remain where they belong in the folder hierarchy.

Force folders and files to follow orders

By default, folders and files arrange themselves alphabetically, but you can force your own arrangement by preceding the file names with numbers, such as 1, 2, and so on. If later you want to insert a new file into the system, you can use 1.1, 1.2, etc. This method can be especially helpful if you're working on a project that involves files you want to keep in a particular sequence.

So much of our work is done on computer these days that it's worth a bit of effort to keep your systems organized and streamlined. If you save even a few moments each time you access a record or return to a document, over the course of a day it adds up. Over a week, you could save enough time to knock off work an hour early!

Save time and trouble with technology

There's a steady stream of new technology products and programs designed to make life easier for small business owners, so any book on this topic will be almost immediately out of date. For that reason, I'm going to mention only a few products here that will save you time dealing with computer issues. However, I invite you to regularly visit this book's companion website, WorkingFromHomeUpdates.com, where I'll keep you up to date on the latest clever and convenient gadgetry for business organizing!

Here are a few ways technology can help:

Keep your books with QuickBooks

Bookkeeping is a huge task that's been made considerably easier with accounting software like QuickBooks, Peachtree, and others. Even so, entering receipts as you accumulate them can be awfully time consuming and it's easy to miss some. Make it simpler by dedicating one of your credit cards exclusively for your business and using it for every business purchase you possibly can. Then, when you receive your statement, simply match the list with your receipts and enter the items into your QuickBooks from your credit card statement. You're sure to capture all your purchases that way.

Theoretically, downloading the information from your bank directly into QuickBooks is even simpler. However, I tried it and found it not as easy as you'd think, and my QuickBooks consultant says I'm not alone! Give it a try if you like and if it works for you, it's that much less you have to do manually.

By the way, you can find QuickBooks tutors and QuickBooks ProAdvisors online, and many accountants have someone knowledgeable on staff to get you set up and to help out when needed.

Care for your customers

Every small business needs some sort of contact management system. You need one place to keep the information you gather on customers or clients, colleagues, and suppliers so you can take action based on the data you collect. The only practical way to do this is on your computer since almost any type of paper system will become quickly outdated as phone numbers, e-mails, and addresses change.

A computer database will let you sort the data in multiple ways in order to analyze trends and uncover opportunities. You can make notes of customer preferences, comments, and problems; then schedule follow-ups at appropriate intervals.

You can use software such as ACT!, Goldmine, or Salesforce, which are specifically designed for these purposes. Or you can use your own Outlook or Google database, though it won't have the sophisticated and integrated systems that contact management software has built in.

Communicate with your customers

If you're using, or plan to use, e-mail, newsletters, or other communication vehicles to stay in touch with your customers, you'll want to use a service such as Constant Contact (ConstantContact.com), AWeber (AWeber.com), iContact (iContact.com), among others that include a list manager. These services are set up to manage e-mail distribution to large numbers of recipients for what's called "permission-based" marketing. In compliance with spam-prevention regulations, they require that recipients indicate their conscious decision to join your mailing list by checking a box or confirming an opt-in message. Most ISPs won't allow mass e-mails, so if you want to build your contact list for Internet marketing, you'll need to subscribe to one of these e-mail marketing services.

Pay *all* your bills online

You may already be paying bills online for those vendors whose websites are set up to do so. But, did you know you can pay *anyone* online? It's not difficult to set up with your bank. To pay a bill all you do is enter the payee, amount, and date to pay, and the bank sends an *e-check*. The names of those you pay regularly stay in the system. You'll be told the date the check will reach the payee and given a transaction number for confirmation. You can pay your bills in no time, with no check, no envelope, and no postage!

Protect your passwords

〉 Password manager software

Passwords can be a nightmare to keep up with, and though most sites have a reset mechanism for forgotten logins and passwords, it can be easy to manage them with a program like Roboform (Roboform.com) and other password managers. These programs automatically create a list of your websites and store your logins and passwords, so you click only once on the name of the site and the rest happens like magic.

If you wish, most of them will generate a unique, complex (mixed case, mixed alpha-numeric and special characters) password for every site you visit. Even though security experts warn us not to use the same password for multiple sites, many of us do because otherwise we can't remember them. With a password manager you don't have to remember anything because it fills in the passwords for you! Roboform comes in an encrypted online version, a version that resides on your own computer and one you keep on a flash drive for automatic login on any computer.

Password manager programs usually also include a feature that fills in forms with names, addresses, credit card numbers, etc., for online purchases, event registrations, and the like. This saves time and ensures you don't make a typo entering credit card numbers.

〉 Spreadsheet

You might prefer keeping a log of websites and passwords on a simple spreadsheet, like Excel. If you do this, I'd strongly recommend you attach a password to the document so that only someone with the password can open it. Or you could keep the document on a removable flash drive.

〉 Notebook

If you're looking for a non-technical method, address books work well. They're already divided into alphabetical sections so it's easy to look up website names. However, they don't offer much security.

Other recommendations

In addition to the tips above, I'd like to share some general thoughts about using your computer for business.

〉 Use a dedicated computer

Trying to operate your business on a family computer is asking for trouble. Others will need to use it at the same time you do, settings you depend on will be changed, and sooner or later some critical file will be deleted. This is no place to economize.

〉 Don't automatically stick with the mouse that came with your computer

Most likely, you'll use your computer constantly. Try different styles and shapes of mice until you find one that fits your hand comfortably. If you have any sort of neck or shoulder problems consider a "trackball" style that allows your arm and hand to remain stationary, while you use only your thumb to move the pointer. This style eliminates the need to lift your entire arm every time you move the pointer.

〉 Consider a laptop even if you don't think you need your office to be portable

Unless your work is extremely graphics-heavy or requires exceptional computer capabilities, you can probably find a laptop that's powerful enough for your needs. You never know how your business will evolve and it's awfully convenient to know you can have *all* your information with you no matter where you go. Theoretically you can access everything on your home desktop through LogMeIn or GoToMyPC; however, you'd still need a reliable Internet connection and some other computer to reach it. When you're at home you can connect your laptop to a large monitor and separate keyboard so it functions just like a regular desktop in everyday use.

⟩ Get a computer case that's airport security friendly

A case that unzips flat, with all accessories on one side and only the computer itself on the other, will let you send the laptop through airport screening without removing it from the case. It's quicker and there's less risk of it being left behind in a bin at the security station. Just search "airport friendly laptop bag."

⟩ Have contingency plans

If you live in a place where storms and power outages happen regularly, buy an "uninterruptible power supply." For around one hundred dollars one of these units can provide you peace of mind and five to ten minutes of immediate backup power—sufficient time to save your work and shut down your computer properly.

If it's just your own home that's being disrupted have a plan for an alternative workspace as discussed in the section on offsite offices.

⟩ Backup your files

Back up…back up…back up! If you lose all your data, it will be a disaster. We all know that even though they're more reliable than they used to be computers still fail. Depending on how heavily you use your computer, you should back up your files *at least* once a week, and preferably every day.

There are different ways to do this, requiring different degrees of user involvement. You can back up to an external hard drive with a few clicks at the end of each day or you can subscribe to a completely hands-off program that will back up to the Web every five minutes with *no* action on your part. Use whatever's right for you BUT do use *something*.

Organize Other Office Operations

"Here are the minutes from our last meeting: Marty wasted 12 minutes, Janice wasted 7 minutes, Carl wasted 27 minutes, Eileen wasted 9 minutes..."

Don't waste valuable time with inefficient and ineffective procedures. And don't waste other people's time either!

Make meetings meaningful

Many solopreneurs with a corporate background automatically resist meetings. That's because they've been subjected to many that didn't accomplish anything useful. Now that they're working for themselves, they may still resist meetings, but for a different reason. Now, time is money. Meetings take time from projects they're working on, and that may cost them money.

On the other hand, it's good to get out of the house once in a while and maintain contact with live human beings, so sometimes you'll want to schedule meetings. Meetings can indeed be useful for the following purposes:

1. Move a promising relationship from accidental (as in a networking encounter) to purposeful (as in we can do business together or learn from each other).

2. Set a friendly and informal tone for brainstorming.

3. Ensure that you have each other's undivided attention (with a phone meeting, you never know what the other person is really doing).

4. Jointly create something like a presentation or content outline where continual editing without actually seeing the final product may be awkward.

Just make sure your meetings have a purpose that is to everyone's benefit. Here are some tips to help make that happen:

Announce the agenda

Always let people know the purpose of the meeting, the items that will be discussed, and the meeting length. Issue a detailed agenda indicating the exact amount of time allotted to each discussion topic. This technique will help you control the meeting and provides you a neutral way of preventing someone from monopolizing the discussion. You can simply say you need to hear from everyone within the time limit. If you really want to catch people's attention, schedule your meeting for an unusual length of time, say 40 minutes. They'll assume the meeting will be tightly run and won't be a waste of time.

Simplify Scheduling

There are a number of online meeting schedulers that totally eliminate the annoying back and forth of meeting date negotiations. Some of the most used are TimeBridge (TimeBridge.com), Doodle (Doodle.com), and Schedule-Once (ScheduleOnce.com).

These wonderful time savers allow meetings to be scheduled with a single e-mail. The meeting host indicates his or her availability on the program's calendar and sends it to the invited attendees, they add theirs, and the software automatically finds the times that work for everybody. The host confirms the date to all and it's done!

They're all easy to use and they're all free! Some offer advanced features for a modest charge.

Consider conference calls

No matter how worthwhile the meeting, it still takes time. Even if the meeting itself is short, getting to and from the meeting location can use up more time than people can spare. Once you're past the getting-to-know-you stage with the other participants, many people are perfectly fine holding a meeting by conference call or other online meeting and screen sharing tools, some of which are *free!*

Use the phone efficiently

Schedule specific times for phone calls

Keep a running list in your planner/calendar of calls you need to make as you process paper, e-mail, and other work throughout the day. Set aside particular times of day to make these calls and return calls from others. Let your voicemail take calls at other times so you can work without interruption.

If you want to reach people, a good time is usually just before lunch or just before quitting time. People are frequently in their offices then and unlikely to prolong a conversation unnecessarily. If you prefer to just leave a message without getting involved in a conversation, call after hours or during lunch.

Process incoming calls first

Listen to voicemails you've received before making outgoing and return calls so that you're prepared to respond to questions or to ask questions of your own during the calls.

Plan outgoing calls

Group and prioritize your outgoing and return phone calls. Before you begin, check your files and contact management database to see if there are any issues pending and jot down the main points you want to cover. This will keep the call from wandering and will be especially helpful if you get a person's voicemail. If possible, have the person's record in front of you when you call so you can update it during the call. Otherwise take notes in your phone log book or planner/calendar and transfer them later.

If your call is likely to be lengthy, it's a good idea to send an e-mail in advance mentioning the topic to be discussed and suggest setting up a phone meeting. Then both parties will be available and prepared. When you do call, ask immediately if it's a good time to talk. It's embarrassing for both sides if you jump right into a discussion only to be told the other person can't talk just then. If it's not a good time, ask if you can leave a voicemail or send an e-mail, so that the task is off your to-do list.

Manage voicemail

When picking up or leaving voicemail, use a phone message log book where you can note the date and time and content of the message you've left or received. Personally, I like the Adams® Write 'n Stick Phone Message Pad that makes a carbonless copy. One copy of the message remains in the spiral notebook as a permanent record while the other has repositionable adhesive on the back that allows you to place it in your planner or tickler file for action or follow-up.

When leaving a message, explain what the call concerns and suggest a time to call back. Say your name and phone number at the beginning and again at the end of the message. Repeat your phone number at a pace that would allow a person to write it down; that's what they'll be trying to do!

Consider adding a comment to your own voicemail greeting explaining that you return calls at such and such times, and offer an alternative if you have one (maybe your cell phone number) for urgent matters. Most people will hesitate to interrupt you unless it really *is* urgent.

Document discussions

Keeping notes on all significant incoming and outgoing calls may seem like overkill, but when recollections differ you'll be glad to have something to refer to. When action is required on your part be sure to enter it in your planner/calendar before you forget. And when action is due from someone else, make a note on the day it's due to follow up.

Conclude calls with a recap

Restate the action steps you've agreed on before you end the call. For example, after a conversation during which you arranged a meeting with a client, you might say, "So I'll meet with you at your office at 10 a.m. tomorrow and we'll spend three hours on your project." This takes just seconds and can save you time down the road by making sure everyone's on the same page. When you're talking with someone on the phone, you don't know if they're giving you their full attention or are multi-tasking. If you don't remind them what they've agreed, they may not think of it again.

Organize books and reference material

Your home office may have unintentionally become the default destination for all the nonfiction books in your home. If they're now crowding you and taking space you need for other things, it's time to pare them down and get them organized.

Sort and select

Gather all the books, binders, manuals, reference material, notes, etc. Weed out anything you no longer find useful. This may include old encyclopedias, college textbooks, outdated computer manuals, gifts from friends and family you know you won't read, or books on subjects you are no longer interested in.

Sort them into boxes according to categories that make sense to you. As you sort, try not to get distracted by individual books, just put them in the correct box and keep going. Once the sorting is finished select the ones you want to keep. You'll be able to see how much room you'll need to store them.

Check around the house to see if you already own suitable bookcases or shelves. If you do, decide where in the office they'll fit. If you'll need something new, take measurements. If space is tight try framing a window or doorway with floor to ceiling shelves. This can be a good way to create storage where there doesn't appear to be any.

Reorganize and re-shelve

Determine appropriate categories and put the books you refer to most often on the most accessible shelves. Arrange the categories, and the books within categories, in the way that makes the most sense to you: by subject, title, author, or any other way that will enable you to easily find what you're looking for. It really doesn't matter how you organize your books. The goal is to eliminate those that are just clutter and store those remaining in a way that is practical and functional for you.

Outplace the books you won't keep—relocate them to other places in the home, give them to others who can use them, donate them to an organization whose members will enjoy them, sell them online, or if all else fails, just throw them out.

Track product inventory

If you sell products and have samples or inventory to store, shelving units are usually the best way to keep them visible and convenient. Cabinets are another possibility, depending on the nature and size of the products. Whatever you choose, be sure the area is well lighted, easy to access, and can be kept at an appropriate temperature. Plan where items should go based on how frequently you'll need to access them and how difficult they are to handle. Store awkward, heavy items where you'll be able to lift and move them. If you have small items, keep similar ones together in containers rather than standing them individually on shelves. Clear stacking drawers are ideal for organizing different types of very small items.

Organize products according to broad categories and apply labels to the shelves so you'll know where to look for things. If you have sales literature, keep it together with the related products. If you use containers, choose clear ones that allow you to see the contents and the amount you have. You don't want to discover at the last moment that you're out of something, nor do you want to buy more than you need because you don't remember how much you have.

To keep a handle on quantities, it's a good idea to create a list of products and the amount on hand. Update this list as you sell so you always know when it's time to reorder. Determine your reorder point based on how quickly products move and how quickly you receive your shipment when you place a new order.

Part II
STAY MOTIVATED

**Create an environment
and mindset that keep you
enthusiastic about your work**

Be Your True Self

"Even though I work from home, it's important to dress appropriately. For conference calls, I wear my best bathrobe. For sales calls, I wear my lucky slippers. And on casual Fridays, I go commando."

*After all, I **am** a professional!*

Many people stumble upon their careers. They didn't necessarily intend to be a teacher, or a sales representative, or a personnel manager. Nonetheless they find themselves filling that role. Perhaps it was the result of family expectations, or a subject they liked in school, or a job that happened to be available at the time they were looking.

As the years goes by they mold themselves to fit the job, but eventually they realize it's not who they really are. They'd rather be doing work that lets them be who *they* want to be, rather than who *their job* wants them to be. That's one of the major benefits of being in business for yourself—you can be your *true* self.

Pursue your passion

Spend your life doing what you love, and the day-to-day ups and downs will be much easier to manage. However, understand that passion for your business will ebb and flow. When passion runs low, ramping up perseverance can help carry you through.

> ❯ Regularly remind yourself of the reasons you started your business.

> ❯ Create a vision board of images, quotations, and goals that motivate you to stay energized and focused.

> ❯ Keep your vision in mind as you work. It's what initially fueled your desire to have a business of your own, so adopt an attitude of total commitment toward the success of your business.

> ❯ Start each day doing the things you enjoy most about your work.

> ❯ Get involved with organizations whose missions align with yours.

> ❯ Connect with and learn from others who are on the same journey that you are, but further along the path.

Welcome challenges

Running a business is tiring, stressful, and challenging. Small business owners are required to wear many hats, all at the same time. Regardless of how much you enjoy your business, it can drain your energy and motivation. Recognize that by being in business for yourself you are learning new skills and taking risks that most people aren't willing to do. It's not easy. If it were, everybody would be doing it!

> Join or create a small mastermind group of action-oriented people in similar but non-competing businesses. You'll share insights from your unique perspectives and will get advice, support, and feedback that will encourage you to try new things in your business.

> Keep a "Hits & Misses" journal. Reward yourself for hits; analyze and learn from misses.

> Take classes on topics that will help you grow your business. When you take a class or attend a workshop you're exposed to new ideas, tactics and strategies. Go for the content, but also take the opportunity to meet people. Follow up with them afterward; they're interested in growing their businesses, too.

> Write down your goals and review them daily, weekly, and monthly, so that you stay focused on priorities. Be specific and identify measurable endpoints so it's clear whether they've been accomplished. If a priority task is particularly challenging, or you've been avoiding it, break it down, ask for help, or learn the necessary skills to get it done.

Acknowledge achievements

Don't look to anyone else for a pat on the back. When you work from home, you need to be your own best friend. *You* know when you've done a great job; that's what matters!

> **Set short-term goals that you can accomplish quickly**. Long-term goals are also important, but when a goal is far off in the future, it can be too ab-

stract. Short-term goals are more immediate and within reach.

> Accomplish something important first thing in the morning. You'll feel good about your achievement and you'll be motivated for the rest of the day.

> Celebrate success and reward yourself when you sign up a new client or complete a project.

> Re-read the successes in your Hits & Misses journal when you need a boost.

Maintain the Right Mental Attitude

"Hello, Maintenance? Could you send someone up to the 14th floor to adust my attitude and install more patience?"

It's up to you to control your own mental state. Don't hesitate to reach out to others for help.

Surround yourself with positive energy

Create a supportive environment

Create an environment that's motivating. For example, listen to music that energizes you. Make your office inviting so that you'll want to be there and will feel good about working.

Develop healthy routines

Being in good physical condition supports having a good mental attitude. Ease into the day with something you enjoy as part of your daily pre-work routine. Start with positive habits and routines. Make physical exercise and a healthy breakfast a regular practice so you'll feel energized the rest of the day. Eat lunch. Get a good night's sleep. Give your body and brain the fuel and rest they need so you can do your best work.

Associate with positive people

Read or listen to motivational and inspirational material. Choose upbeat, happy people as friends and colleagues. Avoid those who seem to attract trouble and want to involve you in it. Don't participate in negativity or gossip.

Focus on your strengths

Your business can become tedious if you have to spend a lot of time on tasks that you don't like and aren't good at. Focus on your strengths and find others to handle the rest. When you're able to do the things you do well and enjoy doing, it's easy to feel positive about your work and your business.

Seek solutions to challenges

Positive thoughts promote a can-do attitude, which helps you find solutions to life's everyday challenges. If something is preventing you from feeling motivated and inspired, determine what it is and change the situation or the way you're dealing with it. Staying bogged down in a problem and not solving it just saps your energy and makes it worse.

Count your blessings

Be thankful you're working from home and not in some cubicle! Remember the reasons you started your own company. Remember the things you didn't like about working for someone else. Can't remember? Recall them, write them down, and add them to your vision board. Read them every day.

That gratitude will motivate you to work harder, so you can continue to work from home. Create a habit of gratitude and you'll maintain a positive and energetic mindset. Even if you're having an off day there's so much to be thankful for. Take the next step and volunteer with a group that serves those who are less fortunate.

Reward yourself

Rewards are not only motivating; they're a way to pat yourself on the back for your accomplishments since there's no boss around to do it for you.

Dangle a carrot

Some tasks are just tough to get through. Instead of trying to avoid them or letting them affect your attitude, decide to reward yourself when they're done. Anticipating a reward helps you stay focused on achieving the end result, especially if you defer that reward until you accomplish a particularly challenging task. While it may be true that a job well done should be its own reward, a little extra incentive doesn't hurt.

Create an incentive program

Make a rewards list. Identify specific rewards to give yourself and post the list where you'll see it every day. It should include both big and small treats to help you stay positive and inspired. Reserve the most significant rewards for those days when *nothing* goes right, and keep reminding yourself that at the end of the day, that treat is waiting for you.

If you don't reward yourself for small victories you'll quickly burn yourself out and become less productive. This isn't being selfish; you need it and deserve it!

Stay on top of your game

Many people enjoy friendly competition with their co-workers. That's what performance contests and rankings are all about! When people work alone they may miss that. So redesign the kinds of competition that kept you motivated in the workplace in ways that suit your new solopreneur status. You can compete against industry colleagues and/or against yourself! Here are a few suggestions about how you can do that.

Compete against colleagues

> Place Google alerts (Google.com/alerts) for your competitors' names as well as commonly used industry phrases. Google will send you an e-mail whenever those words appear on Web pages, news releases, articles, or blogs. This means that you'll always know when items about your industry or your competitors appear on the Internet. Place a Google alert for your own name, too!

> Subscribe to industry publications to keep up with the latest developments.

> Visit competitors' websites to see what they're saying and doing. Analyze the techniques they're using.

> Join competitors' mailing lists to learn what they offer their customers.

> Join and comment on business-oriented social media sites so that you become known as an expert.

> Join industry associations to take advantage of educational content and networking opportunities.

> Attend industry educational and social functions and meet the leaders, movers, and shakers. Learn from them.

> Visit industry trade shows to compare your products and services, and upgrade if necessary.

> Join a mastermind or other accountability group that has no members in direct competition. You'll be motivated by their accomplishments and raise your own game so you won't be left behind.

Compete against yourself

> Set **"S-M-A-R-T"** goals for all your business activities. (See the *Set Goals and Priorities* section for an extended discussion of S-M-A-R-T goals.)

Specific – clearly defined

Measurable – quantifiable

Action oriented – can be accomplished by *doing* something

Relevant – to your business objectives

Time-limited – done by a deadline

> Analyze results vs. goals for each time period and adjust accordingly, always trying to improve on your current performance.

> Optimize your website for ease of navigation and for search engine friendliness. Make sure it compares favorably with others in your industry.

> Develop and execute an effective social media strategy if that's appropriate for your audience.

> Create and distribute an e-newsletter to stay in touch with current and prospective customers. Offer an incentive for response in each issue to measure effectiveness.

> Keep statistics on everything you do—e-mails, blog posts, teleconferences, articles written, newsletters, networking events—everything. Analyze results and challenge yourself to steadily increase your numbers for activities that work best.

> When working on projects, set short deadlines to push yourself to greater efficiency. See if you can turn out more or better work in less time.

> If it presents a new challenge, assume a leadership role in one of your industry organizations.

Just because you're working alone doesn't mean you can afford to let yourself drift into complacency. Competition is motivating to most of us, so stay up on what everyone else is doing and make sure you stay even with, or ahead of, the pack!

Consider the consequences of failure

If you don't stay motivated enough to get your work done you may have to go back to working for someone else. Keep a list of all the reasons you wouldn't want to do that. Make another list of all the qualified people you know that don't have a job and aren't able to find one. Do you want to be competing in today's job market?

If you need extra motivation:

> Paste the mortgage bill in front of you.

> Keep your family's photo in front of you.

〉 Create deadlines

There's nothing like time pressure to get work cranked out. When you create a short timeline, the more there is to get done, the more you will do. This only works, however, if you have a way to hold yourself accountable.

〉 Find an accountability partner

Make commitments about what you will accomplish to someone who'll give you strong negative feedback if you don't do it. Some partners attach a monetary penalty to non-performance, such as donating to a cause they don't agree with. This accountability partner could be a family member or a business associate, business coach, or a mastermind group member, if you belong to one. It should be someone who would be disappointed in you if you don't perform.

Savor the Social Aspects of Business

"When you say you want to be 'just friends' do you mean Facebook friends, MySpace friends, Twitter friends, Buzznet friends, LinkedIn friends...?"

Remember when romance was tricky and friendship was simple?

Foster friendships

Just about everyone you meet is someone you may be able to do business with or refer to someone else. This network of business associates helps fill the space that coworkers used to occupy.

One of the biggest adjustments people face when working from home is the loss of a built-in social network. It's natural to develop deep personal connections with people you spend time with every day—sometimes for years. You collaborate, you share experiences, you hear about and perhaps meet and get to know each other's families. You look forward to sharing ideas, victories, and frustrations. You become part of each other's lives. When you work in a traditional office setting, you take this camaraderie for granted, and for many people it's one of the things they come to enjoy most about their job.

When you're accustomed to being with others all day working alone can be lonely. You're on your own when it comes to thinking, planning, and brainstorming. There's no one to share ideas with, consult, or ask for advice. No one to recognize and compliment you for a job well done. No one to lift your spirits when you're feeling low. Many people realize the social component of business is one of the things that helped them stay motivated and enthusiastic about their work.

It's true that most people who work from home don't feel isolated once their business is up and running. Eventually their days fill with clients, suppliers, and business associates. Still, it's easy to lose touch with the latest developments in your field and to miss office camaraderie and long-term, collaborative social relationships. Some people just work better when they have others around to keep them motivated and moving forward.

It's good to know there are many ways you can create similar business friendships, even though you're working from home. There are lots of organizations filled with people wanting to connect with you.

Be businesslike

Join your local chamber of commerce. These organizations are business-oriented and provide the opportunity to connect with others in the business community. Since membership is usually open to anyone, you'll meet people from every kind of industry. Chambers usually hold monthly meetings and a number of less structured events where everyone mingles. They may also offer presentations by members or guest speakers on business topics or community issues. You can learn from these speakers and potentially become one.

If you live in a large city consider joining a small, "neighborhood" chamber of commerce. It's easy for a solo professional to get lost in a chamber that has thousands of members and caters to multimillion-dollar companies. But smaller chambers tend to be friendly, informal, and filled with "solopreneurs" like you. It's easier to make personal connections at small events and programs geared to the needs of small business owners. Word-of-mouth referrals are common.

Be of service

Join a service organization such as Rotary, Lions, or Kiwanis. The purpose of these organizations is to serve the community, and working on a common cause with others of like mind provides an excellent opportunity for genuine relationships to develop. Since most of the members are in business, they often establish long-term business friendships with one another as a welcome benefit.

Be professional

Join your industry's professional or trade association. These organizations provide excellent opportunities to exchange information and ideas and to keep up to date with industry practices. Look for other professionals in your industry who are not directly competitive due to geography or specialty, and see if you can join forces in some way. You may be able to refer business to one another or complement each other's products or services.

Be where the action is

Join a group that your ideal clients already belong to. The easiest way to meet potential clients is to go where *they* go. So if your ideal client is a creative person who needs help managing the financial aspects of his or her business, join an organization whose members are writers, designers, and photographers—even though *you* may be an accountant.

Be one-of-a-kind

Join a category-exclusive networking group. This kind of organization exists specifically to exchange business referrals among its members. Two well-known groups of this kind are BNI (Business Network International; BNI.com) and LeTip (LeTip.com). Since only one person from each type of business is permitted, when there's a referral for that type of business, it's yours!

Members take turns making presentations about their businesses so that the others understand what they have to offer and what kind of clients they're looking for. Members are also expected to look for opportunities to promote one another's businesses and to produce referrals at weekly meetings.

Be a lady (or gentleman)

Join a women's business organization. As the number of women in business has grown, many women's business groups have sprung up to provide networking and professional support. Some are focused specifically on exchanging referrals; others are more casual and offer socializing and general business camaraderie. Most include education and professional development as well as networking. Some are active in political issues that affect women.

You may not realize that some of these groups welcome men as members, too. And if you're a man in an organization whose membership is predominantly female, you definitely will be remembered!

Be active

Whenever you join a group, volunteer for a committee and participate in activities. Find some area you're genuinely interested in, and you'll find others who share your interest. Working on projects in small groups always makes it easy to get to know people. Change committees every year to meet different members.

When you meet someone interesting at an event, suggest you meet for coffee or lunch and learn more about each other's businesses. Such meetings are a bit more personal and tend to move the relationship forward. Come prepared with specific questions or comments, or ask how you can get involved in whatever it is your new acquaintance is doing that interests you. Most people will be pleased that you reached out to them.

Be a partner

Create an ongoing relationship with someone who adds value to what you do. For example, a business coach and a professional organizer/productivity specialist might serve the same clients in different ways.

Develop a speaking event package that includes several topics and speakers, inviting people whose businesses complement yours to join you. Each person contacts organizations he or she knows to find bookings for the group.

Find other work-from-home professionals and start an informal monthly get-together to have lunch and talk about whatever is of interest.

Be selective

Associate with individuals who have positive and optimistic attitudes and who will lift your spirits and help out when you have a problem. Stay away from negative people. It's unlikely you'll turn them around and they'll just drag you down with them.

Almost everyone can benefit from the mental and physical stimulation that comes from working with others. Even when you're on your own, it's possible to create these business relationships; you just have to make it a priority.

Demonstrate accountability

A boss who keeps a close eye on you is highly motivating, as perverse as that may seem! But when you work for yourself, by yourself, there's no one you're naturally accountable to on a day-to-day basis. Of course when you make a commitment to a client you follow through; however, a general absence of accountability can lead to a loss of discipline, and it takes discipline to be productive when working from home.

To revive the habit of accountability, start making commitments to your business associates. Having someone else's expectations to live up to is a great motivator. Making commitments will encourage you to be more disciplined in your work and in setting daily priorities.

Demonstrating accountability produces a valuable side effect in that you'll be seen as someone who fulfills promises—someone who delivers what and when you say you will. This will instill tremendous confidence in those who have the ability to refer work to you.

> When you've had an in-depth conversation with someone, promise to get back to him or her with some piece of useful information—and do it within a few days!

> Talk about your goals and plans with others.

> Identify and commit to accountability partners who will lose a little respect for you if you don't accomplish the goals you said you would.

> Keep a time log of your activities throughout the day. Keeping a written record of how you spend your time will help you spend it wisely and get more done, just as keeping a written record of what they eat has proven helpful in encouraging people to eat more wisely and lose weight.

This log doesn't have to be fancy or complicated. In fact, don't spend a lot of time creating your log instead of doing your work! For a computer time tracking tool, try Paymo (Paymo.biz). They offer a completely free version that's geared to freelancers and solopreneurs. If you prefer a paper log, use a planner/calendar that's formatted into days and hours so you don't have to do it yourself.

Receive recognition

When you work from home, you have no boss to say "thank you" and recognize you for a job well done, so do it for yourself! The challenge is that we're often quick to focus on what we intended to do that we *didn't* get done. If you tend to be hard on yourself, write down at least one thing you did well each day in your Hits & Misses journal. Perhaps you finally made that difficult decision, got started on a project you've been putting off, or stuck to your resolution not to visit Facebook once all day!

Here are a few other ways you can receive the recognition that motivates you.

> Volunteer with a community organization that can use your expertise. Choose one whose mission aligns with yours.

> Get involved on a committee or accept a board position in your professional association or trade organization.

> Teach at an adult education center or community college.

> Become an expert in some aspect of your business and become a speaker, or write a book.

> Do something no one else has done.

> Start a new trend; create a new paradigm.

> Find out about high profile events and conferences in your industry and submit speaking proposals.

> Hire a publicist.

> Recognize the accomplishments of others and send notes of congratulations.

Notable accomplishments in any of the activities above will bring you not only recognition but also prestige. Many people would like to earn respect in their fields; some know what they need to do in order to make that happen; few actually *do* it. If you're willing to do what it takes, the rest follows naturally.

Enjoy the Journey

"If I stop to smell the roses, then all the other flowers will expect me to smell them too and I'm just too busy for that!"

Besides, the last time I stopped in the garden there was that unfortunate incident with the gnome.

Spruce up your workspace

One of the prime benefits to jumping off the corporate treadmill and into your own business is that you have more choice over everything, including your office.

Express yourself

In most of today's larger businesses there's not a lot of room for individuality. Offices tend to have the same look within a given company, using the same equipment, the same supplies, and more or less the same procedures. That's because the people holding the jobs there are just passing through. The *company* is the constant. "Your" office isn't really yours; you're just using it while you happen to work there.

When you work from home, however, there are no such constraints. You get to decide how your office looks. If you love a particular color, paint it on the walls. If you don't want to furnish your home office with regular office furniture, which might make it look and feel too commercial, look for file cabinets disguised as end tables, coffee tables, or sofa tables. Manufacturers are now making lots of furniture specifically designed to blend in with home décor.

Indulge in patterned file folders. Office supply stores now stock all kinds of decorative and colorful paper goods. You might not be able do that in a corporate office, but in a home office you can do whatever you want.

Put up framed pictures of your family, friends, pets, etc., to brighten your workspace. If music creates a productive environment for you, download a free Internet radio site like Pandora (Pandora.com), which is customizable with your favorite kind of music.

Entitle yourself

Don't try to make do with an old table banished from elsewhere in the house when what you need is a proper desk with file drawers. Find a file cabinet you like. Get a comfortable and ergonomically correct chair for computer work. Splurge on attractive office supplies that are stylish and make you feel successful. If something doesn't work properly, get it fixed.

Add plants, artwork, or other items that motivate and energize you. Surround yourself with things that stimulate positive, productive feelings and will put you in the best frame of mind.

Every work-from-home solopreneur deserves a workspace that satisfies his or her soul in both functionality and aesthetics. If you love the space you work in, you'll be more focused, creative, and productive.

Measure more than money

Money isn't everything, but it isn't the root of all evil, either. If you're in business to make a profit, the money your business brings in is simply a measure of how successful it is. As a business owner you have more control over the amount of money you make than you ever would as someone else's employee. But don't let making money consume your life. Work smart and enjoy yourself along the way.

Beyond the basics of running a profitable business, here are a few suggestions:

> Analyze the return on investment (ROI) on your business activities and your customers. Concentrate your efforts on the 20 percent that yield 80 percent of your profits. You may be able to make the same profit with a lot less work.

> Outsource must-do activities for which the ROI isn't sufficient for you to spend your own time. Support another small business owner!

> Constantly upgrade your products and services to justify premium positioning and pricing. Make more profit with each sale.

> Always be looking for new revenue streams: books, seminars, public speaking, licensing or franchising, Internet marketing, or coaching others.

> Be open to collaborating with related businesses. Two heads are usually better than one.

> Remember, it's profits that count—not revenue. You can't make up in volume what you lose on each unit!

Value variety

If you start to run out of enthusiasm and inspiration for your work or find that you're easily distracted and not able to stay on task, do something different. Just because you work from home doesn't mean you have to be stuck in your office all the time. In fact, you should make a point of including a variety of activities in your day.

A change of scene gives you the chance to reboot, refresh, revitalize, and recharge. When you return to work, you'll see things with new eyes and feel more innovative and productive.

Here are a variety of ideas to keep you energized and motivated.

Exercise

Exercise offers numerous benefits for everyone. Not only is it good for your health, it's good for your brain. Activity improves circulation, increasing the oxygen supply that helps generate fresh ideas. If your day involves mostly "brain work," it's good to give your mind a break now and then and shift the focus to your body. Especially if you're at your computer most of the time, it's important to get up and *move* at least once an hour or so. It's easy to become so immersed in work that you entirely lose track of time. If that tends to happen to you, set a timer to remind yourself to take a break.

Stand up, stretch, climb up and down a couple of flights of stairs, take the dog for a walk, water the plants, or do a few crunches on the balance ball. A little exercise will help keep the muscles you don't use (back and legs) from getting so stiff and the muscles you *do* use (eyes, neck, arms, and fingers) from being overworked.

At some point in your day, try to exercise for a longer period of time. A brisk walk, a trip to the gym, or time on the treadmill will do a lot to help keep your energy up and your weight in check.

Pace yourself

Alternate between work that requires intense mental effort and less demanding tasks that don't call for the same level of concentration. Read those articles waiting for you, de-clutter your desk, or update your contact database.

Change the view

Work in a different location for a while—a different room in the house, the back yard, a coffee shop, at the library, or in the park.

Don't eat lunch at your desk, grabbing a bite between phone calls or other tasks. Take a real lunch break; leave your office and eat in another part of your home. Sometimes you'll get new ideas by looking at things from a different perspective, literally.

Get out of the house

Take a scheduled break and leave your workplace, as you would if you were working in a traditional office environment. If you have a dog, this is a win-win since you'll both get a break. Otherwise run an errand or two, work in the garden for a bit, or walk around the block.

Just be sure to get back to work when your scheduled break is over!

Forget about business

Don't let yourself become one-dimensional, living and breathing work all the time. Remember that one of the reasons to be in business for yourself is to set your own schedule. Clear your mind completely. Take an afternoon off to indulge in a hobby or other personal interest. Read a book, go to a museum, see a movie, visit a friend, volunteer for a cause that touches your heart.

Be sociable

An important business-social activity to fit into your schedule is some kind of networking. Attend a meeting of one of the business organizations you belong to, or try out a new one. Meeting new business-minded people is fun with a purpose. It's easy to make small talk because everyone wants to chat about his or her business, and it's understood that that's why you're there. Even if you don't encounter a prospective client, it's likely you'll meet someone interesting or hear some idea you can use.

At least once a week, meet someone for lunch. This is a great way to add a personal component to your relationship with a client, business associate, or someone you've met at a networking event. You'll broaden your range of contacts, learn about someone else's business, and exchange ideas. You may even discover common interests or new ways to work together, though that shouldn't be the primary goal. The primary goal is to give yourself a mental, physical, and social break, so just relax and enjoy the downtime.

Teach a class

Consider passing on what you know by teaching classes at a junior college, at a continuing education center, or in a series you arrange and schedule yourself. Regular, challenging interaction with a room full of adults who regard you as an expert will keep you on your toes! You'll definitely sharpen your skills as you prepare course material and the questions and comments from your students will give you new ways of looking at your work.

Working from home comes with many perks and benefits, but staying in your office by yourself all day will eventually suffocate you and your business. Adding variety to your day will help keep you motivated and productive.

Part III
GET THINGS DONE

Discover ways to set, prioritize, and achieve your goals

Pick Goals and Priorities

"Don't dress for the job you have, dress for the job you want. I want a job that let's me kick some butt!"

Be as specific as possible about your goals, so you'll know exactly what you need to do to achieve them!

Generate goals

The first step in shaping or growing your business is to decide what you want to achieve. Goals you set should be designed to move your business forward. If you don't have a destination in mind, how will you know if you're headed in the right direction? The easiest goals to set are those that are layered—long-term, mid-term, and short-term. You need to be able to translate your long-term goals into actions you should be taking right now. So, if you want to increase annual sales by 10 percent, how many new orders a day is that?

Most small businesses have multiple goals. However, it's counterproductive to focus on more than two or three at a time and you should make sure these are complementary, not conflicting.

Long-term goals

Long-term goals are usually strategic and expressed at the "results" level—what you want to have happen. For example, let's say your long-term goal is to be known as an expert in your industry within five years. A *complementary* goal might be to have also written a book, since authors tend to be regarded as experts. In contrast, a *conflicting* goal might be to develop a new product within that same time frame. While the inventor of a new product might also be regarded as an expert, the time and effort spent on creating a new product might keep you from being able to write the book, and if your new product doesn't catch on it won't position you as much of an expert.

Mid-term goals

Mid-term goals are more tactical in nature. What do you need to have accomplished by a year from now to be on track to hitting your long-term goals? In our example, if you want to be seen as an expert, your mid-term goals could include being the chair of an important committee in your professional association within two years. You might aim to be a speaker at four industry conferences within three years. You could plan to submit your book manuscript for publication within four years.

Short-term goals

With short-term goals, you're deciding what actions you will take within the near future (this month or this quarter) to ensure you'll achieve your mid-term goals. Now, it's clear to see you need to join that professional association right now and find out which are the most prestigious committees. You might join Toastmasters within the next three months to sharpen your speaking skills. And you could start gathering material for your book by interviewing one expert per month to learn what industry trends your potential readers will be most interested in five years from now.

You'll recognize certain things about the way the goals above are described. They follow that formula using the acronym "S-M-A-R-T," which I introduced in the last section.

Specific—clearly defined

> Be very specific about your goals and put them in writing. Just writing them down will cause your thinking to become clearer.

> Use "commitment" language. Don't write, "I want to"; write, "I will." This tells your subconscious that there is no choice. It will help you attract the people and situations you need to achieve that goal.

> List the benefits you'll enjoy once you've accomplished your goal. This will keep you focused when you're tempted to let things slide a bit.

Measurable—quantifiable

> Choose goals that can be measured. Measurable goals are motivating because you can track progress toward reaching them.

> Measurable goals are concrete; either you did it or you didn't.

Action oriented—can be accomplished by *doing* something

> Action is the engine that drives goal achievement because taking action is within your control.

> When you write your goal, include an action plan that will ensure your goals are achieved. You should feel confident that, as long as you follow the action plan, results will follow.

> Anticipate challenges you'll encounter and plan how you'll overcome them.

> Take daily action toward achieving your goals.

Relevant—to your business objectives

> Goals must contribute to the success of the business, to move you forward and spark positive change.

Time-limited – done by a deadline

> Goals without deadlines are only dreams. Worthwhile goals aren't accomplished overnight; you'll need to make time and expend effort to make them happen.

Pick priorities

There will always be more items on your to-do list than you can ever complete. You don't have infinite time or resources. It's frustrating and stressful, but you just have to admit it's simply not possible do everything you'd like to in the time you have. Prioritizing is the only solution.

If you don't consciously set priorities, you let whatever comes up determine how you'll spend your time. You can work very hard without accomplishing much that's important. Setting priorities forces you to evaluate each item on your task list and make a conscious, thoughtful decision about the best thing to do. By clarifying your priorities you'll actually accomplish more in less time. You'll work smarter instead of harder.

There's a well-known concept that supports this. It's called the Pareto Principle, or the 80/20 Rule. The general idea is that 80 percent of our results come from 20 percent of our efforts; 80 percent of our income comes from 20 percent of our clients, etc. In countless ways, most of what we do each day has little impact on our lives and a few things have major impact. Therefore, you want to focus 80 percent of your attention on the 20 percent of things that make a difference. The trick is to identify the most important 20 percent that should be your priorities! Over the years, experts have devised a number of strategies commonly used to help identify priorities. Consider trying one or more of the following:

1. "Covey Quadrants" System

This was created by Stephen Covey, the author of *The 7 Habits of Highly Effective People*. It's based on evaluating the *importance* of a task versus its *urgency*. An issue is *important* if it helps you achieve your goals. It's *urgent* if you must do it immediately or you can't do it at all. Tasks are categorized by being placed in one of four quadrants:

Q I **Important & Urgent**	Q II **Important, but Not Urgent**
Q III **Urgent, but Not Important**	Q IV **Not Important & Not Urgent**

Items in Q I are tasks that are very important to achieving your goals *and* have a deadline that must be met immediately.

Q II tasks are also projects that are important to achieving goals; however, deadlines and consequences aren't breathing down your neck this minute. This remoteness can make it easy to put these tasks off, so it's important to keep them moving or urgent problems may arise and shift them into Q I.

The items in Q III and IV are the day-to-day busy work that can consume great amounts of time if you're not paying attention. When some things aren't going to get done because your workload exceeds the hours in the day, these are the things to let drop.

The tasks in Quadrants I and II are the ones you should spend most of your time on.

2. "A-B-C" System

This is a simple and direct way of prioritizing:

"A" High Priority Tasks

> Immediate or critical for survival

> Require special effort or concentration

> Vital to the needs of your customer or business associate

> High positive or negative consequences

"B" Medium Priority Tasks

> Everyday, routine work

> Need to do, but not critical and can be postponed if necessary

"C" Low Priority Tasks

> Low priority paperwork, reading

> "Nice to do" if you get the time

> Let's face it: Most of these won't ever get done

You can further prioritize within categories, such as A-1, A-2, B-1, B-2, and so forth. In truth, most "C" tasks remain forever undone simply because you can't get to them, but as long-range goals come into view, some may graduate to "B."

3. "Value vs. Effort" System

With this system you weigh the value of the task against the time and effort required. Those tasks with a high reward-to-effort ratio rise to the top of the list and those with a low reward drop to the bottom. Ask yourself these questions:

1. What's the value of this task on a scale of one to ten?

2. What's the level of effort required by this task on a scale of one to ten?

3. What's the value compared with the level of effort?

Rank according to the degree to which the level of value exceeds the level of effort. For example:

Task	Value	Effort	Difference	Priority Rank
1	10	10	0	2
2	4	5	+1	3
3	6	10	+4	5
4	1	3	+2	4
5	10	4	-6	1

Prioritize those tasks with the greatest payoff compared to the time and effort required.

Manage Your Time

"Time management is a myth! If I had control over time, I'd still be sixteen and weigh 90 pounds!"

Wouldn't it be wonderful if the "backspace" key could do that?

People say that time is money, but that's not exactly true. You can always make more money. You can get a raise or a better-paying job. You can invent a widget and sell it. You can get more customers to buy more widgets. You can increase the price of the widgets. You cannot, however, make more time.

While it's possible to add extra hours to your work day, do you really want to be all work and no play? Even if you love what you do and don't mind working long hours, you're not going to be doing your best work if you've been at it for twelve hours nonstop.

What is usually called "time management" could just as accurately be called "workload management." You need to fit your workload into the amount of time you have. Since everyone I know has more work than time, the only way you'll do that is to use your time wisely and not waste it.

How much time do you waste?

Studies show that the average business person wastes one hundred fifty hours per year—*nearly three hours per week*—searching for misplaced items, such as phone numbers, documents, and computer files! Even worse, workers in small and medium-size businesses spend half the work day on unproductive tasks. They're busy, but spending too much time on things that don't count at the expense of things that will make a difference in their business.

How wisely do you spend *your* time? Time management isn't about working faster; it's the practice of spending 80 percent of your time on the 20 percent of activities that are most important.

Manage time as carefully as you manage money

When it comes to spending money, most people have to consider how much something costs. You can't see a beautiful home for sale and simply decide to buy it without regard for the price. No matter how beautiful something is and no matter how much you'd like to own it, if you don't have the money you can't buy it.

It shouldn't be any different when it comes to spending time. No matter how worthwhile a project is and no matter how much you'd like to do it, if you don't have the time, you can't do it.

Treat the hours in the day in the same way you would the money in your pocket. You must budget sufficient time for the must-do items and what you have left has to cover the less important items. This means that there are some things you simply cannot afford to do. Time isn't an unlimited commodity, so spend it wisely.

Become more time-attentive

Raise your level of time consciousness.

> ❯ Use an analog clock, whose moving hands show the passage of time.

> ❯ Set a timer to develop a more concrete sense of time. You'll be surprised how quickly an hour goes by.

> ❯ Learn how long it takes to complete regular tasks.

Treat yourself like a client; analyze your own time management ROI

Keep a time log for a week. Use a time tracker on all your work activities, just as you would if you were working for a client.

Time management and productivity experts love time logs, though people often resist. At some level, most of us know we're not managing our time as well as we could. Here are three reasons to do it anyway.

1. **You become engaged in your own productivity.**

Becoming more productive doesn't just happen; it takes work. It doesn't happen until you're actively working to get control of your time management.

2. **You get a painfully accurate picture of where your time is going.**

Most people think they know how they're spending their time, but when they actually see the data and confront the truth, they recognize that changing a few small habits can make a big difference.

3. **Simply keeping the time log makes you manage your time better.**

In the same way that keeping a food log helps people lose weight, keeping a time log instantly improves the situation. Why? Because no one wants to write down that they wasted forty-five minutes following some irrelevant thread on the Internet! Just making yourself accountable can often break you of a bad habit.

> Analyze how you're spending your workdays. Patterns will emerge that will help you get more done during your workday.

> > Would better planning reduce the amount of time you spend putting out fires?

> > If you didn't allow interruptions to derail you could you get more work done?

> > Are you spending most of your time doing the handful of high priority items that really matter?

> > If you were paying someone by the hour to do what you do, would you think the charges were reasonable?

Upgrade your time management techniques. If you've been using the "I do what I feel like doing when I feel like doing it" method of time management, consider replacing that with some of these ideas.

> > Before doing anything, ask yourself how much time you're willing to invest. Block only that time in your calendar and stick to your time budget.

> > Enter specific times in your planner to do specific tasks

> > Prioritize: Work on the most important and urgent tasks first.

> Reprioritize and reschedule tasks throughout the day.

> Look for time-wasting activities in your business and eliminate them.

> Use short bursts of intense focus to maximize productivity.

> Always confirm meetings and appointments the day before; you'll save yourself time and lost temper if someone forgot to cancel.

Plan for productivity

Don't mistake activity for results; just because you're doing something doesn't mean you're being productive. What makes a day productive isn't just crossing things off your to-do list; it's working on the really important things in your business. In order to be productive, you need to manage your time and your workload. That means planning. And that means faithfully using a planner/calendar.

Use a planner/calendar

The single most effective action you can take to become more productive is to use a planner/calendar. I use both terms, "planner" *and* "calendar", because planning work and scheduling appointments are actually two different functions that you should incorporate into the same device. You should enter all time-specific commitments, both business and personal (the *calendar* function), then plug tasks from your to-do list into the times that are left (the *planner* function.) If you haven't been using a planner/calendar consistently you'll be amazed at how much simpler and more productive your life can be.

Once you start using a planner, you're rarely faced with a blank page when you turn to a new day. You'll have already entered time-specific to-do items, follow-ups, meetings, errands, and phone calls on the days you need to address these tasks. When you can see the day is about to overflow, you can start re-prioritizing, rearranging and rescheduling if necessary to avoid creating a schedule that you can't possibly execute.

Keep only one

Schedules are much too busy these days to rely on memory alone. You need one single place to keep track of all meetings, tasks, projects, and follow-ups. Keep *all* time commitments, whether professional, personal, or family, in a single calendar. Otherwise, sooner or later you'll forget something or double-book yourself.

You may currently be using several calendars: one on your phone, another on your computer, a third in a little notebook you keep in a purse or pocket, and perhaps a family calendar hanging on the wall. As long as your information is scattered in lots of different places, you'll find it difficult to be truly organized and productive. You need one single calendar you can trust to have all the information you need to know where you're supposed to be, and what you're supposed to be doing at any given time.

Keep it with you

The best planner/calendar is one that can capture thoughts and tasks wherever you happen to be, so you'll use it consistently. Therefore, you should choose something, whether paper or electronic/digital, that's small enough to have with you all the time.

Keep it your own way

As soon as you get into the topic of planner/calendars, the question comes up, "paper or electronic?" Whichever you use to do your planning, there are advantages and drawbacks. Most people have a sense of which they prefer, but if you're undecided or considering a change, here are some pros and cons.

> **Paper**

Advantages

> Familiar; no learning curve

> Non-intrusive for note-taking during meetings

> Infinitely customizable

> No electricity or recharging needed

> Provides a written history

> Lots of room to take notes

Drawbacks

> There's a limit to how much information you can keep with you.

> Recurring events must be entered individually.

> Even a medium-size notebook may be too large to keep with you all the time; therefore, you can't easily check your calendar or add new tasks as they come up.

> Making schedule changes is cumbersome.

> Numerous changes can look messy and be hard to decipher.

> Uncompleted to-do items must be re-written every day.

> Considerable searching may be required to locate an entry.

> **Electronic (specifically, a smartphone that syncs with a computer)**

Advantages

> All your information on your cell phone, which you probably keep with you anyway

> Calendar, planner, telephone, contact list, to-do lists, navigation function, as well as lots of other useful features, all in one device, all at your fingertips, all the time

> Small enough to keep with you all the time for reference and additions

> One click enters recurring events, ensuring they're not forgotten

> Alarm reminds you to take action

> Easy to update changes in addresses, phone numbers

> Easy to arrange to-do items in empty spaces around time-specific commitments

> Easy to rearrange tasks to accommodate changes in schedule or workload

> Searchable for phone numbers, appointment dates and other bits of information

Drawbacks

> Need to keep battery charged

> Phone keyboard can be small and awkward to use

> Difficult to get a sense of the entire month's activities

> If you lose your smartphone you lose everything

You might find the best way to go is with some combination of paper and electronic. Some people keep their calendars in Outlook or Google Calendar, and then print it out for a longer range view.

⟩ Non-traditional methods

Sticky notes

If you're a devoted user of sticky notes, go ahead and keep using them! But consolidate and organized them by sticking them on the pages of your paper planner. You'll be reminded of tasks each day just as if your notes were written on the page itself, and the notes will be easy to move to other pages if your schedule or workload changes.

It's convenient to have a little pad of sticky notes with you all the time that you can jot notes down on. Just remember to transfer them to the appropriate page in your planner before they're misplaced.

Index cards

The forerunner of sticky notes, index cards, are an alternative you can use to note tasks, projects and follow-ups. You can devise your own system to manage their status, or use tools available through Levenger (Levenger.com). Levenger offers index cards pre-printed with lines, grids, contact information, or to-do lists, along with ways to display them standing up so they're a visual reminder of what you need to do. They sell a tiered wooden stand for your desk or a traveling version that collapses flat to slip into a tote bag or briefcase.

Index cards come in a variety of colors and some are even backed with repositionable adhesive.

They're easy to carry with you and cards can be arranged according to priority, date, location, company, project, or any number of other ways you might find useful.

Keep everything in it

Your planner needs to be the one-stop-shop for everything you have ever promised anybody, including yourself, that you would do. It needs to be a trusted system that contains your meeting schedule, projects, task lists, status notes, follow-ups, and cross-index to your tickler file. If you're conscientious about keeping your planner up to date, you can completely relax and know you won't overlook anything.

Keep lists

Using lists effectively is the secret to success. Important thoughts occur to us spontaneously throughout the day—things to do, to follow up on, to buy, to talk with someone about. If you don't capture them immediately, they're gone. Keep your lists in one place and keep that one place with you all the time. Don't let yourself develop the habit of jotting things down on random pads of paper. I've seen too many people frustrated by notepads all over their office, each one with the top half-dozen sheets of paper covered with lists of various sorts. The result is they don't know where to look next. What has already been done and what has been overlooked are lost in the visual clutter of half-completed, partially crossed-off lists.

You may decide to separate your list into tasks of different categories, but at least if everything is in one place you'll know exactly where to look when you are at the store, on your way to a meeting, ready to return phone calls, or when you find yourself with a few extra moments to get something done. Ideally, that one place with all your lists should be in your planner/calendar! That way, you can quickly transfer a task from one of your lists right into your calendar if you see you have an open slot in your schedule.

While I'm in favor of lists in general, I do make a distinction between "someday" lists that capture every task, hope, dream, and intention that ever crossed your mind and real "right now" to-do lists—tasks you actually schedule into your planner to do on a specific day. Everyone has lists filled with things that will probably never get done—they're not essential, they require some resource that isn't available, or the time isn't right. Some items on your "someday" list may eventually become "right now" items for a real to-do list, but continually reviewing lengthy lists and feeling inadequate because you can't fit everything into your current schedule is self-defeating.

Keep time

Real to-do lists should be made up of those tasks you actually *will do* in the near future or on a specific date further out. But when planning your schedule, glancing down a list can be misleading. A single entry that takes one line to write could take two *minutes* (a phone call) or two *hours* (a proposal). Therefore, when you add an item to your to-do list, it's important to include an estimate of how much time to allow for that task.

Write your estimate next to the task so you'll know where to schedule it into your planner/calendar. Your estimates may not be very accurate when you first begin. However, as you complete tasks, note next to your estimate how long it actually took you. Do this for a few weeks and you'll become much more skilled.

If you realistically estimate how much time each task will take, you can schedule it on a day when your calendar shows you'll probably have time to do it. But be aware that organizing your time does not mean scheduling every moment of your day. Most time management experts suggest planning only about 50 percent to 75 percent of your day to allow for underestimating how long tasks will take and to accommodate work you didn't plan for.

You should review your planner/calendar on a weekly basis so you can distribute your upcoming workload in a way that will enable you to accomplish everything you need to do. If it becomes clear that you've scheduled more work into a given day than there is time to do it, you can reprioritize, renegotiate, or reschedule.

Schedule specific times

While lists are helpful for remembering what you need to do, they're not at all helpful for actually getting things done. If you don't decide exactly *when* you will complete a task, it's likely to just stay on the list, waiting for you to think of it at exactly the time you happen to be free to do it. Since that rarely happens, the result is often a list of tasks that just keeps getting longer and longer. Let your calendar/planner help you turn them into real to-do items and get them done!

A planner helps build your workdays automatically by structuring them around specific tasks that need to be completed by specific dates and times. First enter the time-specific commitments; next start adding tasks from your to-do list based on their due dates. Take note of how much time the tasks will require; then enter them into available time slots just as if they were time-specific appointments.

This technique is a valuable time-management tool because it accomplishes two important things. It provides an early warning system to alert you when you have scheduled too much into a single day. It also eliminates the question, "What do I need to do today?" Your planner has automatically scheduled your day.

Sort out the steps

Due dates have a way of sneaking up on you before you know it. If you're facing a large project, break it into small steps and enter them in your planner at a pace that will get the whole project completed on time.

Breaking out tasks in this manner is a practical way to get things done since it's highly unlikely that you'll be able to find three solid hours to work on a large three-hour project. It's much more likely that you'll find a series of hour-long time slots here and there in which you can accomplish small steps that will add up to a completed large project.

1. Identify *every* tiny step that will be necessary to complete the project.

2. Place them in the proper sequence.

3. Estimate how long each step will take (then add 50 percent!).

4. Ask someone who has done a similar project for a sanity check.

5. Schedule the steps in reverse order into openings in your calendar, working backward from the deadline date.

6. Set the deadline date a bit earlier than it actually is. Most projects encounter unexpected issues along the way, so start *much* sooner than you think you need to!

Managing tasks in this way will keep them moving ahead without wearing you out. When you've put in the amount of time allotted, you can put the project aside without guilt. Take a break. Walk around for a bit and come back refreshed and ready to tackle the next piece of work. When you organize your work using this technique, you'll find you're not only more productive, but you'll probably do better quality work, too!

Do your to-do list

Have you ever said, "I just can't seem to get my to-do list done!"? Do you think if you just got organized enough you could get everything done? Don't count on it.

The average person has so many things on that list that if he or she did nothing else but work on those things—didn't go to work, had no personal life, *nothing*—and added nothing *new* to their list it would take approximately ten weeks to get it all done! What does that tell you? It tells you *no one* gets everything done from an endless to-do list!

Money, space and time have something in common. They're not unlimited commodities. You only have so much, and you have to make do with that amount or give up something to make more. There are only twenty-four hours in a day, and while you can definitely accomplish more by increasing productivity through good time management, there's only so much you can squeeze into those twenty-four hours!

Think about it. Anything on your to-do list will take time, so if you want to do it, you need to find time for it. If your days are already full, you'll have to *save* time by doing other things in a faster or smarter way, or *open up* a time slot that would otherwise be filled with some other activity. This requires constant decisions about priorities and requires a realistic look at your to-do list itself. You should use the same formula when you make your to-do list that you use for setting goals—remember, "SMART?"

Make a SMART to-do list each day

Your to-do list should be made up of **S**pecific things that can be **M**easured (either you did them, or you didn't), are **A**ction oriented, **R**elevant to your objectives, and **T**ime-limited. It isn't the right place to list all your wishes and dreams. It's not a storage spot for all your most creative ideas. Yes, have lists for those things, but don't call them to-do lists and don't expect to accomplish them when you already have twenty-four hours of SMART things on your to-do list that need doing right now.

Actually, I recommend that instead of creating lengthy "to-do" lists you enter specific tasks that you will do at specific times in your planner/calendar. By changing from writing lists to scheduling actions you'll accomplish much more!

Think of your to-do list in a new way:

> A to-do list should be just that...a list of things that you *plan to do*. Planning requires that you choose high-priority activities, estimate how long they will take to do, decide when you will do them, and enter them as *actions* in your planner/calendar.

> Keep your daily to-do list short. Decide which two or three tasks absolutely MUST be done by the end of the day. Fit your to-do actions around the time-specific commitments already in your planner. Identify specific times during the day when you'll complete those important tasks and make an appointment with yourself by actually entering them in your calendar. Include only tasks you can realistically schedule into your day, allowing time for the unexpected.

> List your to-do items as specific actions you'll take. If your schedule allows you an hour for your marketing project, decide what exactly you'll do in that time. Will it be to draft copy for a sales page, will it be to identify potential joint-venture partners, or will it be something else? What, exactly?

If your project is large, break it down into segments that can be done in sixty to ninety minutes and spread them out over however many days are necessary to get the job done. Eliminate other things if you have to.

> As you're planning your day, prioritize your to-do actions and handle the most important one early in the day. Pick the one that will make the most difference to you, your business, and your clients and focus your attention there. Tackle that one first thing in the morning and get it done, before other issues grab your attention. That way, if your day gets disrupted, at least you've accomplished the most important thing.

Don't even look at your e-mail or listen to voicemail until after the most important task is done. Discipline yourself to stay focused and avoid distractions throughout the day. Don't be tempted to finish up all the little tasks that are nagging at you so that you can "really concentrate" on that important one.

> When you have something new you need to fit into a day that's already full, reconsider your priorities, delay something, delegate something, or delete something.

It's perfectly acceptable to postpone an item that's on your to-do list if it isn't urgent or important. Move it to another day when you can squeeze it in. However, if you find that you keep forwarding it for weeks, re-evaluate if it should be on your list at all.

Don't demoralize yourself with an unrealistically long to-do list that you'll never get done. As with most things, the 80/20 rule applies. 20 percent of the tasks on your list will contribute to 80 percent of your success. The secret lies in determining which items really deserve to be on your list!

Prevail over e-mail

While e-mail is an essential tool in business today, un-scrupulous marketers have made it an annoyance by filling our inboxes with spam. In addition, well-meaning friends who aren't as busy as we are send us bits of useless information, stale jokes, and links to irrelevant articles. As a result, even though most of what we receive each day is welcome and important to our business, e-mail has acquired a bad reputation.

At the same time, e-mail has become a socially accept-able addiction. It's something easy to do when you want to get away from something else—a tiresome project or a difficult challenge. It appeals to the same psychological mechanism that draws us to the refrigerator, to smoking, to drinking, or to surfing the Internet.

E-mail is seductive because it holds the excitement of the unknown. Something interesting could be waiting—a message from someone you'll be happy to hear from, even a problem that needs taking care of, but something that will surely distract you from whatever it is you should be doing.

Managing the avalanche of daily e-mails is the number one complaint of office workers these days. However, if you're working solo, you need to learn to deal with e-mail because there's no one to delegate to—you're it! Experts recommend the following techniques for controlling e-mail:

Eliminate the unnecessary

Unsubscribe from newsletters, chat rooms, and other on-going communications that aren't important or useful. Create filters for messages you don't want to see and people you don't want to hear from so those e-mails never reach your inbox at all. They'll be diverted to your spam folder.

Remember, legitimate e-mail you wouldn't want to miss may occasionally land in your spam folder. So check it every day or two to make sure something hasn't been delivered there by mistake. Permanently delete the rest.

Don't "check" e-mail

Instead, commit to "processing" e-mail at designated times throughout the day, for a specific period of time. This approach calls for a completely different mindset. You are not just looking to *see* what is there; you will actually *handle* what is there.

For most people it's sufficient to process e-mail no more than three or four times a day. For example, if you decide to process e-mail at 9 a.m., noon and 4 p.m. you can spend the rest of the day doing useful work. Impose strict limits on how much time you spend on e-mail while you have important projects waiting. Set a timer if you need to.

Consider adding a line to your e-mail signature block mentioning that due to your workload you now are answering e-mails at (whatever times you are), and offering your cell phone number if a matter is urgent. Most people will stop expecting immediate responses, and few will interrupt you if it isn't truly urgent.

Evaluate e-mails expeditiously

How many times have you opened, reviewed, and closed the same e-mail? Those messages are taking up too much of your time and attention especially since nothing is actually being accomplished. In the meantime, as they continue to sit there they turn into a list of nagging to-do items that overwhelm you each time you look at them. What a time waster—opening each one again to remind you what you need to do! And as new e-mails flood in, the older ones sink further to the bottom of the list until somebody grumbles or you realize it's too late to deal with them at all.

It's better to handle e-mail messages as they come up— which means you have to evaluate them and decide what to do. The choices you have are limited:

1. Delete

Delete without opening e-mails from unknown persons, with subject lines you're not interested in, and anything else that looks like spam.

2. Open and skim

> Scan for credible senders and read them next.

> If the message doesn't relate to anything you're currently working on or imagine you'll be working on in the future, delete it. If it's an offer to participate is something time-limited, and you know you're not interested, delete it.

> If the message is for information only and won't require action, read it quickly, take note of anything important, and *archive* the message.

Yes, my suggestion is that you *archive* the e-mails you decide to keep instead of filing them. Like most saved material, you'll probably never refer to 80 percent of them again, so don't bother creating an elaborate filing system for e-mails you've read. The 20 percent you may wish to refer to in the future can be quickly found by your e-mail program's search function. If your e-mail program doesn't have a built in "Archive" folder, simply create one yourself and sweep all your e-mails in there once you've read and dealt with them.

3. Do it (in two minutes or less)

If the message calls for some action on your part, ask yourself if you can do it in less than two minutes. If you can, just do it. If it will take longer, defer it.

4. Direct or delegate it

If the message is better handled by someone else, direct it to that person. Add an explanatory note if needed. After you direct it elsewhere, archive the original message in case you need to follow up in the future.

5. Defer it

If the action required is something only you can do, and will take more than two minutes, decide its priority and note a to-do action in your planner/calendar on a specific date. If you're using a computer calendar paste the entire message into that day, so you'll be reminded of the context. The original message will probably include phone numbers and other information you might need. Drop the original e-mail into the Archive folder.

6. Drop it into the Archive folder

Since you never know which messages contain some piece of information you'll want to reference again, and computer storage is practically limitless, why not keep everything that's not obvious trash? Just drop it into your Archive folder, where it will wait until you need it. If and when that time comes, a quick search on a key word or phrase, or the sender, will deliver the relevant messages.

Silence the signals

Turn off the "new mail" alert on your computer. Better yet, completely avoid e-mail distraction by keeping your e-mail program closed except during those times you've scheduled yourself to process it.

State the purpose in the subject line

If the recipient of *your* email needs to take action, make it clear in the subject line so the e-mail isn't overlooked or misunderstood. If the e-mail is for information, state the main point. Later, when either of you needs to find this e-mail again, it can be quickly identified by just the subject line.

Don't process e-mails first thing in the morning

If you want to make progress on important projects, do them first thing in the morning *before* looking at e-mail or listening to voicemail. Any given day's e-mail is sure to contain issues that will lead you astray. E-mail and voicemail can almost always wait for a couple of hours until you take care of the one or two really critical tasks that must be done right away. If a *real emergency* arises, you can be sure someone will call you on the telephone rather than sending you an e-mail.

Don't use your inbox as a to-do list

Continually reviewing a list of e-mails you haven't dealt with is a complete waste of time—the equivalent of going through stacks of paper on your desk over and over, reminding yourself of things you need to do without actually *doing* them.

Move them to a "pending" folder or better yet, paste them into your Outlook or Google electronic calendar on the day you've decided to act on them. Leaving them in your inbox is guaranteed to make you feel overwhelmed.

Banish the backlog

I've seen inboxes with hundreds of e-mails in them, and heard stories of people with thousands! What can you possibly do if that's your situation? Here's an extreme solution: Take a deep breath and start over.

1. Delete any message more than a month old. By now, the person has either forgotten they sent it, has given up on you responding to it, or the issue has long since been resolved.

2. Of those remaining, sort by sender. This will make it easier to identify the ones you need to respond to. Do your best to answer the messages that are still relevant. Delete the rest. Granted, it's not ideal, but what else can you do? You may have deleted something important that you shouldn't have, but the result is no different than if it continued to sit ignored in your inbox. Either way, you wouldn't have seen it and wouldn't have done anything about it.

3. Be prepared to apologize to those who berate you for such an extreme action (*if* you choose to tell anyone what you've done). My guess is the critics will be few; more will be bedazzled by your boldness!

Remember, e-mail is a tool—not your job

Your to-do list is more important than your e-mail. Keep things in perspective and don't let e-mail take over your day. If you're not careful, you can waste large chunks of time without much to show for it. Accept the idea that ignoring some e-mails may be necessary given your other priorities.

Consider adding a notice to your signature block that states the times of day you process e-mail and suggests calling if the issue cannot wait. This will lower expectations that you'll respond immediately to every message. Most people will think twice before interrupting you with a phone call unless the matter really is urgent.

Don't overlook e-mail's benefits

However excessive and frustrating it may be, e-mail remains the tool of choice for business communications. It's an essential part of your everyday productivity. And there are plenty of good things about it. E-mail:

> Allows you to assign rules, alerts or filters to pre-label or sort messages so that important ones come to your attention and unwanted ones are immediately deleted

> Saves endless rounds of telephone tag when you're trying to share information or reach agreement

> Allows you to leave and receive messages when it's convenient for *you*, without interrupting the other person

> Replaces meetings held just to keep everyone informed

> Reduces telephone interruptions

> Documents details and agreements

> Is searchable by sender, topic, or any other criterion

In truth, e-mail can save lots of time and trouble if you don't become a slave to it. The key is to manage it, just as you do every other aspect of your work.

Round up resources

When you work for yourself, by yourself, the demands on your time are overwhelming. You simply can't do everything you want to, or even *need* to. As your business grows, this becomes more of a problem. However, many solo professionals want to remain solo and don't want to take on the responsibilities and expense of employees. What then?

Get help

You don't have to do everything yourself. In fact, you probably shouldn't. The simplest way to maintain your solo status while still growing your company is to have a great network of expert resources. There are some tasks that will save you time, energy, and money if they're handled by a freelancer or independent contractor. Administrative tasks, for example, are often easy and inexpensive to outsource. And the time you free up in your schedule can be spent doing those things you're good at and enjoy, ones that will contribute to the bottom line.

Build a support network

You may not have the convenience of the built-in support network that you would in a traditional working environment, but you can still have reliable help. And unlike the colleagues who just happen to work at the same company, you can *choose* who you want to work with when you build your *own* network.

Develop relationships with other small business owners to whom you can outsource the activities you don't have time for, aren't good at, or don't like doing. Identify the tasks you'd like someone else to do, and as you're out meeting people in the ways suggested in the *Foster Friendships* section, take note of those who might make good colleagues. Get to know them. Ask them to work on small projects with you, or for you, and see how it goes. Once you feel confident in their competence and compatibility, use them regularly. Develop genuine personal relationships and be appreciative of their help.

Build a referral network

Someone you'd consider to be a good colleague for yourself would be a good referral to others who need the same type of help. Be generous in your referrals; those you refer business to are likely to return the favor when they can. In addition, they may well be looking for someone like you to outsource *their* tasks to! Before long you may have created a virtual company of sorts—an informal group of solo professionals working independently but together.

Build a professional network

Every small business owner should seek out professionals who specialize in small businesses. Sooner or later you'll need a banker, lawyer, insurance agent, and accountant— and if business is successful an investment adviser! One of the pleasant side effects of membership in business organizations is that you're likely to meet these people naturally. Create your professional network from those who are knowledgeable in their fields, of course, but also from people you like and trust and who get good reviews from others. Meet with them on a regular basis so that when something comes up, they know your business and you have a solid foundation to work from.

Build an overflow network

There may be times that a business opportunity presents itself when you are just not able to take advantage of it. Perhaps you're already completely booked, or the skills needed are a bit outside your core expertise, or the client is geographically inconvenient, or you're just headed out on vacation. Depending on the nature of your business, you may want to engage someone in your own industry as an independent contractor or a subcontractor. Get to know others who do work similar to yours whom you would feel comfortable recommending or sending in your place. Many people are happy to pay a percentage of earnings as a referral fee in such cases.

Consider a virtual assistant

A virtual assistant (or VA) is someone who handles tasks for you but works from his or her own place of business as an independent contractor, someone you might never meet in person. Communication is via phone and e-mail. VAs work best in an ongoing, one-on-one, collaborative relationship. They usually provide administrative support, often specializing in creative, medical, legal, financial, or technical fields.

Their backgrounds, which often include experience as an executive assistant or office manager in addition to their specific skill set, make them reliable, responsible, and resourceful. They may handle appointments, bookkeeping, customer service, website creation and maintenance, online marketing, or other important but time-consuming tasks for solo professionals. This can be extremely cost-effective since they're paid only for actual time worked.

Consider a professional organizer

If personalized, hands-on help is what you need—someone who can assess your personal situation and offer solutions tailored to your individual way of working—look to a personal organizer. The National Association of Professional Organizers (NAPO.net) has thousands of members across the U.S. and around the world. Professional Organizers can be found in other countries, too: Australia—www.aapo.org.au, Canada—www.organizersincanada.com, United Kingdom—www.apdo-uk.co.uk. Many specialize in business services including organizing, time management, and productivity. Search by location, background, or special skills to find one who can help you. Professional organizers who focus on small businesses have skills and resources to solve problems common to work-from-home professionals. Most professional organizers are work-from-home professionals themselves!

Manage Yourself

"Ever have one of those days when you're not sure whether you're in the zone, out of the box, under the gun, over the hump or behind the curve?"

Then there are other days when you're out to lunch, in a fog, all at sea, or just generally in a mood.

Often, when people speak of *time* management, what they really mean is *self* management. It's one thing to have a knowledge of time management processes and quite another to use them. You must manage your self so as not to waste your time.

Being productive in your home office demands more than just getting organized and staying motivated. You have to get things done. That means understanding your own strengths and weaknesses, being disciplined enough to deal with distractions, determined enough to overcome procrastination, keeping yourself on task, and resisting tendencies to commit to more than you can deliver.

Pay attention to your personal energy cycle

Go with the flow

Some people are night owls; some are early risers. Most people have energy ebbs and flows throughout the day. When your energy level is high is the best time to tackle your most difficult tasks. Even though many time management experts advise getting your most demanding job out of the way first thing in the morning, if you're sluggish at that time it will probably take you longer to produce mediocre results than it would to produce excellent results later in the day.

If networking and high-energy personal interactions are important to your business for lead generation or client meetings, try to schedule them during your "prime time." If you're at your best in the morning, try to set up morning events instead of after-hours get-togethers. Schedule low value activities that don't require a sparkling personality, such as processing e-mails or filling out paperwork, for late afternoon when your energy is low.

Eat well

Your diet has a direct effect on how energetic and productive you feel. Feed your body well and it will respond by keeping you alert and enthusiastic.

Sleep soundly

In order to sustain energy levels throughout the day, get a good seven to eight hours of sleep each night. Consider adding relaxing night-time rituals to your routine such as reading or stretching. Establish a regular biorhythm by going to sleep and waking up at the same time each day.

Plan your workday the evening before so that your mind knows what to expect and your subconscious feels prepared.

Just say "no"

Saying yes to requests from others is the path of least resistance. It's often nice to be asked, and you may not want to disappoint someone who needs your help. However, your time is limited, and it's valuable. Don't allow others to pressure you into spending it on things that are important to *them*. The more willing you are to say "no" to others' demands the better able you'll be to create the life *you* want.

Prioritize

As much as you'd like to accommodate someone else's requests, you have your own priorities. Make sure you're not sacrificing what's important to you.

Schedule short days

It's easy to unintentionally over-commit if we assume that our days will unfold as planned. However, that's rarely the case. Inevitably, emergencies and unforeseen circumstances arise that keep us from being able to deliver what and when we promised. When judging what extra activities you can take on, assume that you'll lose four hours every day to these unexpected developments. If you can add someone's request to your own to-do list and get it done based on four-hour days, by all means say "yes" if it's something you want to do.

Say "no" nicely

Decline without making excuses or going into detail. The more you talk about why you can't do something, the more it invites the other person to try to talk you into it. Try responses like the following:

> ❯ "Let me think about that and get back to you." This is handy if the request takes you by surprise. Nothing says you have to make a decision immediately.

> "I'm sorry, but my plate is absolutely full at the moment."

> "I'm so sorry but I'm over-committed already and just can't take on anything else!"

> "I wish I could, but I'm just not able to do that right now."

Prevent perfectionism

Why do some of the brightest, most talented people put off important projects until the very last minute? They waste precious time busying themselves with unimportant matters until time runs out. Then they hurriedly put together something that's not their best work.

The very people who are the brightest and most talented often set such high performance standards for themselves that they're impossible to meet. Their self image requires that they turn out superior work *every time*, even when it's not necessary. So if a project is new or complex, they hesitate. They're afraid they won't be able to do it well enough.

The irony is they may delay so long that when they finally do get started there isn't enough time left to do the superior work they expect of themselves. They've created a self-fulfilling prophecy. That's the worst kind of self-sabotage! Perfection is an impossible standard to achieve, so seeking it automatically sets you up for failure and disappointment.

Here are some tips to interrupt this destructive habit:

1. Evaluate how much time and effort a project is really worth.

2. Break it down into small steps that are easy to get done.

3. Work backward from the due date to create a realistic timeline.

4. If you can, outsource the steps you don't want to do or don't do well.

5. Schedule in a block of time every week to work on projects.

6. *Just do it!* When you have a project before you, it doesn't have to be done perfectly; it just has to be done.

Some additional thoughts:

> **Strive for excellence, not perfection**

   Unnecessary reworking of relatively unimportant projects can waste time without improving the outcome. Allocate your time and effort in a manner proportionate to the importance of the job.

> **Recognize when good is good enough**

   It often takes 50 percent more effort to squeeze out an additional 10 percent or so of quality.

Prohibit procrastination

With no boss or set schedule, it's very easy for work-from-home professionals to just never get around to tasks they don't want to do—or are afraid they won't do properly. Everyone procrastinates to some degree, but when you own your own business, a procrastination habit can be destructive and self-defeating. Some of the very things you love about working from home—no boss and no set schedule—can keep you from being successful.

In general, procrastination creeps in when a task is:

> Overwhelming

> New, with an unknown path to success

> Something you aren't good at

> Unpleasant or uninteresting

Whatever the reasons, procrastination threatens to overtake the work-from-home professional who isn't on guard. Here are a few strategies you can use to fight back.

When the task is overwhelming

> **Break it up**

Deconstruct large projects into smaller steps. Large jobs can be overwhelming and tempting to put off. But a series of small jobs done over time is more manageable. Identify the small steps that make up the larger whole and build them into your schedule at a pace that will meet your deadline. Once it's clear just what specific tasks you need to do—and when and how you'll be able to do them—you'll be less tempted to procrastinate.

When the path to success is unknown

> **Procrastinate without guilt**

Allow yourself to procrastinate—but set a time limit. Some tasks have unclear starting points. It's tempting to think about them for a while to see if some point of entry presents itself. The fact is, it's often effective to let things sit until they sort themselves out. If you're going to do this, set a time limit. Enter a date in your planner when you will stop thinking and begin working, even if you're still not sure where to start.

> **Start anywhere**

The truth is, it's often easier *not* to start at the beginning. And when you're headed into unfamiliar territory, you often don't have a big enough picture to know where the beginning is anyway. Pick some aspect of the job that seems approachable and jump in. Often momentum will carry you once you get going. Soon you'll see what should come before and what should come after whatever point you started at. The key is simply to *start*.

> **Reach out**

Chances are you know someone who has done some type of similar work and can help get you started. Ask if he or she can give you some insight, ideas, or direction.

> **Remember that most tasks don't have to be done *perfectly*; they just have to be done**

It may be necessary to adjust your personal standards somewhat. Many small business owners are accustomed to excelling in everything they do and approach every task with this mindset. Yet perfection isn't always necessary—or even desirable. If you worry about doing everything perfectly, you won't get anything done. Do the best you can and move on.

When it's something you're not good at

> **Outsource it**

There's no point in forcing yourself to do something you don't really have the skill to do *if* you can hand it off to someone else. It may take you longer than it's worth to do a poor job when your time could be more profitably spent on your core business activities. There is undoubtedly someone else whose business is built on doing exactly what you aren't good at. Find that person!

> Learn how to do it

If the task is an integral part of your work, or something you can't justify outsourcing, accept the fact that you need to take a class, get a tutor, or read a book. Learn what you need to know and get the job done.

When it's unpleasant or uninteresting

> Use the simplest approach and minimum effort that will get the job done.

> Do it first thing in the morning and get it out of the way.

> Decide on a way to reward yourself when it's done.

> Remove distractions that will divert your attention from the task at hand.

> Relocate yourself to more pleasant surroundings to minimize the unpleasantness of the chore.

> Standardize the process so you don't have to think much about it.

> Limit the amount of time you require yourself to spend doing unpleasant tasks. Promise yourself that after fifteen minutes you can stop if you want to.

> If it's a difficult interaction with another person that you're putting off, rehearse the conversation in your head so that you know what you'll say. When you feel prepared, it will be easier.

Procrastination prevents progress, and that's something you really can't afford when you're on your own. If you don't find ways to keep moving forward, your business will suffer and you may soon find yourself *out* of business.

Since everyone procrastinates to some extent, we all know the wonderful feeling of relief once you've finished a task you know you have to do. Stop getting ready to get ready—and just do it!

Deal with distractions

When working alone, and with no one keeping an eye on us, it's sometimes difficult to stay on task. As much as we try, our attention can wander. There are distractions all around us. Here's a list of common distractions to watch out for and what you can do to deal with them.

E-mail

> Turn off that new message alert. It's too tempting to see what's just come in.

> Keep your e-mail program closed until you're ready to process your inbox. Then go through your e-mails quickly as suggested in the *Prevail over E-mail* section until you've responded to the two-minute ones and scheduled the more complex ones. You won't have a huge list sitting in your inbox that you have to scroll through over and over to remind yourself what you need to do.

Telephone

> Don't feel you have to answer every call at the time it comes in. Give yourself some uninterrupted work time each day while your voicemail takes messages.

> Watch your Caller ID if there are some callers who merit your immediate attention.

> Set aside short blocks of time to return whatever calls have come into voicemail.

Paper

> Process incoming paper promptly or you'll find yourself repeatedly looking through stacks to find what you're looking for. Get papers assigned to folders in your current projects or tickler file as soon as possible.

Environment

> When you're working try to ignore whatever's going on around you. Having an office with a door you can close will help. Don't let yourself get involved watching neighborhood activities or the television.

> Put a "Do Not Disturb" sign on the door to discourage others from interrupting your work.

> Arrange your office so you have enough light and there's no glare on your computer screen.

> Limit time spent on household tasks during working hours.

Lists

> Schedule tasks into your planner/calendar as you become aware that they need to be done. Don't keep adding them to a never-ending list. Constantly reviewing to-do lists keeps reminding you of all the things you're *not* doing. Focus on the one item in front of you.

Yourself

> Make sure you're always working on something important. Don't let your mind become preoccupied with something else.

> Get up and move around every hour or so to give yourself a natural break. Your mind and body can stay focused for only so long without seeking a change. Build in breaks before your mind drifts and your body gets restless.

> If you're having trouble concentrating on one task, switch gears and work on another for a while.

> See more suggestions in the *Value Variety* section.

Minimize mental multitasking

Using time efficiently is doing more than one thing at a time when neither of them requires your full attention, such as filing papers while waiting for a conference call to begin, sorting mail while you're watching the news, reading an article while you have a snack, or taking your laptop and cell phone with you so you can work while the car is being serviced. Using time efficiently is a good thing.

Mental multitasking is doing more than one thing at a time when each of them requires concentration; for example, reading e-mails while talking on the phone. You are likely to miss important information from both. Mental multitasking is *not* a good thing.

Managing two mental tasks at once reduces the brainpower available for either task, according to a study published in the journal NeuroImage. A recent study from the Institute of Psychiatry at the University of London suggests that your IQ falls ten points when you're simultaneously fielding e-mails, text messages, and calls—the same loss you'd experience if you missed an entire night's sleep. People who multitask are less efficient than those who focus on one project at a time, according to a study published in the *Journal of Experimental Psychology*.

Recent studies show that on average, it takes three full minutes to regain concentration after switching tasks. Constantly shifting your attention from one task to another steals time and actually reduces your efficiency. Each time you resume a task you have to remind yourself again where you were and what you needed to do next. It's estimated that repeatedly starting and stopping a task can increase the time required to complete the task by as much as five times. You never reach the momentum necessary to perform at a level of real excellence.

Are you convinced yet?

> Try to be single-minded when you're working on a task. Some interruptions are unavoidable, but it's critical to focus your efforts tightly on the task at hand if you want to accomplish it quickly and well.

> Finish a task before starting a new one. Distractions are the quickest way to inefficiency. By concentrating on one single task, you can reduce the amount of time required to complete it by half.

Set up a Structure

**"I work at home too, but you don't see *me*
sitting around in my pajamas all day!"**

*Honestly, when your **dog** starts criticizing you it's time to shape
up!*

Some people may assume that working from home means running your life with complete freedom. However, freedom doesn't mean anarchy! You'll soon find that if you don't structure your workdays you won't get much work done.

When you start working from home it can be a big challenge to structure your own time when you've been used to your employer doing it for you. In your own office, you're in charge of how you do things. If you aren't being as productive as you need to be, it's because your current approach isn't working. Do something different.

The following suggestions will help you get things done while still enjoying the freedom of a flexible schedule.

Divide your day

Remember how your school days were divided into different subject periods? Do the same with your workdays now. Consider the major types of work you have to do you and divide the day into work periods of an hour or so each. Schedule specific time slots to follow up with current clients, strategize to attract new ones, work on major projects, handle administrative tasks, etc. Concentrate on one project or one type of work during each period until that time is up. Then, give yourself a break between tasks, just as if you were changing classes. Walk around or exercise for ten to fifteen minutes then return refreshed to tackle the next type of work.

Workdays are so busy that you won't usually have enough time at one sitting to complete a large project so you're better off breaking them down into smaller tasks. If you allocate certain time periods throughout the day for different types of tasks, you can make progress on all of them. This is more practical than devoting yourself exclusively to one project while all the others are neglected. Of course, there will be times when it's more important to be 100 percent finished with a single high-priority project than to be 50 percent finished with several lower priority ones. When that's the case, make an exception and reallocate your other work to other days.

To squeeze all your activities into an already busy schedule, create weekly and/or monthly calendar templates. Using a spreadsheet, fill in your personal schedule and recurring commitments; then add your recurring business activities. Designate certain days of the week for certain kinds of work. For example, choose a regular time slot that you'll do bookkeeping and send out invoices and another when you'll write your newsletter. Pick a time you'll do social media marketing if that's part of your business. Keep adjusting length and frequency of time slots until you can accommodate everything. Not only will you decide on *specific* times for all of your activities, you'll also make conscious decisions about *how much* time each deserves. As you identify tasks that relate to each type of work, add the specifics to that time slot. You'll quickly see if everything fits or if you'll need to drop or outsource certain activities.

Once you've got a schedule that's running smoothly, consider entering it into your computer calendar so that these recurring time slots automatically appear. If you need to make adjustments occasionally, it's easy to rearrange times on the computer.

Before you know it, the time slots you've reserved for different business activities will fill in with specific to-do actions and you'll have your workdays automatically planned. That's not to say you can't make changes whenever something comes up; that's one of the freedoms of working from home!

Relish routines

The more you can set up your workdays to operate on autopilot, the better off you'll be. Your individual style will determine the exact nature of your individual routines, but the key is to have them. Know what you're going to do each day and jump right in without giving yourself the chance to be distracted by something else you'd rather do.

You may think of routines as boring, but your subconscious interprets them as peaceful and consistent. You'll save time and energy every day by not having to make hundreds of little decisions. When your mind doesn't have to make decisions about small things, it's free to concentrate on more important tasks throughout the day. Following are some good routines to incorporate into your day.

> Create a morning ritual that helps you make that mental transition from being "at home" to being "at work." Every morning, get up, shower, and get dressed. No one works effectively in their pajamas.

> When you work, close the door to shut out distractions and interruptions.

> Take note of personal and household patterns during the day. Work on important issues when your energy and attention are at their peak and household distractions are low.

> Make a list of the two or three high-priority things you want to accomplish each day and don't open your e-mail program until the first one is done.

> Process e-mail only at pre-scheduled times.

> Each time you use a file, quickly go through it and see if anything is outdated and can be tossed.

> As you notice or use the items in your office each day, evaluate them. If they're no longer useful, get rid of them.

> Set up multiple out-of-office appointments on the same day to consolidate travel time.

> If an appointment is made well in advance, confirm it the day before to make sure it's still on the other person's schedule!

> Create a file for driving directions to places you go infrequently so you won't need to ask or look them up again.

> When you finish the priority items on your list, reward yourself.

> Every night create your to-do list and schedule for the following day.

> Take fifteen minutes at the end of each workday to restore order to your office. Leave your office with a clean desk except for the next day's folder from your tickler file. You'll appreciate it the next morning when you walk into an office that's ready for work.

Standardize systems

Harness the power of repetition. Frequent repetition of any task makes it automatic, thus requiring minimal attention. You probably don't give much thought to how you brush your teeth or tie your shoes, because they're now automatic.

Apply this same principal to your office tasks. Once you've determined the best way to complete a task document the procedure. List all the steps from start to finish. Every time you do that task, do it the same way.

> Create templates for everything you do repeatedly, such as developing proposals, sending letters, or answering questions. Create an outline that you can update and reuse.

> Create and use checklists to save time and make sure you haven't overlooked anything.

> Create standard formats for recurring reports.

> Document procedures you do infrequently so you don't have to think them through each item. Keep them all in a "How to..." folder on your computer.

> Also create a "Where is…" computer folder and list where you've put items you use infrequently.

Batch business tasks

Do similar work in the same scheduled block of time instead of bouncing around throughout the day. Dabbling at random tasks here and there significantly reduces your effectiveness at *all* of them. Group like tasks such as paperwork, e-mail, voicemail, etc., and do them in batches. You'll be more productive because you're not asking your brain to constantly switch gears. Every time you change to a new type of work you need time to get yourself up and running again.

If possible, plan your week so that you can consolidate similar activities and schedule them into blocks of time throughout the day and week. For example, reserve one or two time blocks for work on multi-step projects, one for handling financial issues, two or three small blocks per day for e-mail, etc.

When you see a pattern of like actions, locations, or tools try to batch those tasks. For example, batch:

> Voicemail and phone calls

> All types of data entry such as updating customer records or entering information on new contacts

> Out-of-office client visits and miscellaneous errands

> Handwritten correspondence such as thank you notes

Determine *Your* Work/Life Balance

"You should be back at the office. Vacations are for lazy people! What have you accomplished today?"

Isn't it wonderful to get away and completely relax?

Seek "satisfaction"

Work and personal life are rarely balanced in the sense that you can give equal attention to each. Running a business, especially when it's new, will probably be more or less all consuming. On the other hand, there may well be times when your personal life takes over and your business takes a seat way in the back. The important thing is to come to terms with these ebbs and flows and to find a degree of compatibility. Look for big-picture proportions that you're comfortable with based on your own circumstances. Act with intent to balance your work with other life interests. Work-life *satisfaction* is a reasonable goal to strive for.

One of the difficulties work-from-home professionals face is that the success of your business may well have a direct effect on your personal life. If your household depends on the income you're producing, how can you fail to do everything possible to succeed? You want to enjoy a comfortable lifestyle and that requires a serious commitment. If you don't work hard/smart enough you risk losing your business. *Assuming* you're then able to find employment that makes use of your talents and abilities, that new job may require as much time and attention as operating your own business did! And finding a job, any job, isn't so easily done these days.

On the other hand, your own well-being and the personal relationships in your life will wither if you don't nurture them, and that also takes time and attention and commitment. Perhaps the following ideas will help with this genuine dilemma.

Align family expectations

> Thoroughly discuss the benefits and drawbacks of your work with those who are important to you. Be sure they understand the connection between your work and the lifestyle they enjoy.

> Come to an agreement on disruptions to family activities—such things as missed meals and events, erratic working hours, etc. Decide redistribution of normal household tasks if necessary.

> Figure out how to accommodate the need for quiet during non-interruptible work time.

> Set aside time on a regular basis exclusively for family to keep them from feeling subordinate to your business.

> Include your spouse in your business. If your spouse understands your work and what it involves, he or she may be less resentful of the time you spend on it. He or she may also be able to offer ideas you wouldn't have thought of.

Prioritize chores

Just like other tasks, decide the importance of household chores—which ones must be done daily, weekly or at other intervals.

> Consider which, if any, can be outsourced.

> Get agreement on who will do what.

> Don't obsess over having a home that's ready for a visit from *Architectural Digest* on a moment's notice.

Build boundaries

When your office is where you live, it's hard to get away from work. So you need to set boundaries for yourself and others.

Set business hours

> Let your spouse, your children, your neighbors, your clients, and everyone else know what your working hours are. This should help minimize interruptions and distractions.

> Set defined working hours and stop when they're up. Whatever work schedule you establish, be consistent. People will know what to expect and can plan around it.

> Once you've finished for the day, don't go back to work. If you get a great idea, make a note and follow up tomorrow.

Set boundaries to protect family time

Schedule time that's just for the family with no work interruptions.

> If you can create flexibility in your work schedule, give children your undivided attention when they get home from school.

> Buy a clock sign at the office supply store—the type retailers use on their front doors—to indicate what time you'll be available and place it on your office door.

Work around children

Working from home can be especially challenging for people with children, but it's not impossible.

Mind your mindset

> Kids are kids, and they're only kids once; don't make choices you'll regret later.

> Help children understand why you work. Once they're in school, make the comparison between what they do for school and what you do for your business. Your children's job is to go to school and learn; your job is to give them a home and take care of them. You both have to work at your jobs.

Stay organized

If you can only work in short spurts when the children are otherwise occupied, you need to make that time count. Keep your office organized so you know just where you left off and where everything is to get back up to speed. Keep the rest of the house organized, too. Time is in short supply when you have children and it's a shame to waste it cleaning up unnecessary messes or searching for lost items.

Work around them

Work before the children get up or after they go to bed. Work when they're napping. While it may be tempting to take your own nap while your children sleep during the day, you should utilize the quiet time and get to work.

Arrange child care

Most people find they can't allow children to have unlimited access while they're trying to work. You have to accept that you can't run a full-time home-based business *and* be a full-time parent. Figure out how many hours you *can* work and arrange child care during that time. If you can only work three hours a day, so be it. You can get a lot accomplished in fifteen hours a week if you're able to work without interruption.

Here are some ideas to consider:

> If you have a spouse, work when your spouse can look after the children.

> Get supplemental child care to watch the children and keep them occupied—a family member, babysitter or nanny, childcare co-op where parents take turns, day care center, or a neighborhood teenager.

Arrange *backup* child care

> No matter how thoroughly you plan, sooner or later something will happen to your usual child care setup. When that occurs, it is absolutely critical to have a backup plan ready to go.

Set expectations

> Let children know that you're lucky you can work at home instead of having to go away during the day like most people who work.

> Teach them what you expect of them—to let you work and be quiet when you're on the phone unless it's an emergency.

Let them in

> Create a spot for the children reserved for only those times when you're on the phone and need them to be quiet. Stock it with favorite snacks, toys, activity books, and puzzles.

> Set up a part of your office as their "office." Find tasks they can do, have them keep track of their work, and pay them! They'll love being part of your business!

> Take your children with you when you go to buy office supplies or run other business-related errands.

> Have family "study hall" hours in the evening. Instead of fighting the children's need for attention and inclusion, synchronize their needs with yours. School age children usually have some type of homework, so after dinner, clear the table and work together!

> If they don't have homework, they can do some quiet activity—read, color, or work on a project while you do *your* work.

Prepare your clients

If you're on the phone with a client, mention that your children are at home, and ask if you may call back if the children need you. This becomes easier once you have a relationship established, or if your client is also working from home.

Preserve a personal life

When you work from home, there's no natural boundary between being at home and being at work. Like most work-from-home professionals you probably work longer hours now than you did when you worked for someone else. The same technology that offers freedom and convenience to work when you want and where you want makes it easy to work all the time.

Besides, when you love your work, you may not really *want* to stop. However, if you work *too* hard, you risk losing all semblance of a personal life. Do your best to find that combination that brings you satisfaction with both aspects of your life. Remember, your home office is simply one room in your home. Live the rest of your life in the rest of your home.

Conclusion

While you were reading this book, you probably noticed some recurring themes: Plan ahead and make conscious choices about what's important to you. When you started your business, you planned how you would organize and operate it. You need to do the same thing now about how to best work from home. Planning not only enables you to make the most efficient and effective use of your time, but also to anticipate problems and make the best choices about ways to solve them.

As you implement the ideas in this book, you'll undoubtedly be pulled in different directions by outside forces (family, clients, business associates, etc.) and inside forces (procrastination, distractions, conflicting priorities, etc.). One of the great benefits of working from home is that you get to make the decisions that are right for you. I hope this book has given you both encouragement and tools for your success.

Index

About the Author

Elaine Quinn, founder of Space Craft Organizing in Chicago, is an internationally-recognized organizing and time management expert. She is among only 5% of professional organizers around the world who hold the prestigious designation of Certified Professional Organizer®. Elaine is a Past President of the National Association of Professional Organizers-Chicago Chapter, and is currently their Corporate Associate Director. She is a member of the National Association of Women Business Owners and has been quoted in *Success Magazine* and the *Chicago Tribune*.

Prior to her current consulting business, Elaine's 25 years in management positions with Fortune 100 companies developed strong skills in problem-solving, productivity, organization and time management as well as the ability to guide those who reported to her.

As a work-from-home solo professional since 2001, Elaine has helped hundreds of small business owners and other solopreneurs become more productive in their workspaces and workdays.

ATTENTION:
Corporations and Organizations

This book is available at quantity discounts with bulk purchase for business, promotional, or educational use.

For information, please contact
Special Sales Department
Calloran Publishing

SpecialSales@CalloranPublishing.com

CPSIA information can be obtained at www.ICGtesting.com
Printed in the USA
LVOW031022021111

253184LV00001B/1/P